HOW TO SUCCEED IN LIFE

Applying Timeless Principles

BISHOP BEN UGBINE

authorHOUSE®

AuthorHouse™ UK
1663 Liberty Drive
Bloomington, IN 47403 USA
www.authorhouse.co.uk
Phone: 0800.197.4150

© 2019 Bishop Ben Ugbine. All rights reserved.

No part of this book may be reproduced, stored in a retrieval system, or transmitted by any means without the written permission of the author.

Scripture quotations marked KJV are from the Holy Bible, King James Version (Authorized Version). First published in 1611. Quoted from the KJV Classic Reference Bible, Copyright © 1983 by The Zondervan Corporation.

Published by AuthorHouse 12/06/2018

ISBN: 978-1-7283-8204-3 (sc)
ISBN: 978-1-7283-8203-6 (hc)
ISBN: 978-1-7283-8206-7 (e)

Print information available on the last page.

Any people depicted in stock imagery provided by Getty Images are models, and such images are being used for illustrative purposes only. Certain stock imagery © Getty Images.

This book is printed on acid-free paper.

Because of the dynamic nature of the Internet, any web addresses or links contained in this book may have changed since publication and may no longer be valid. The views expressed in this work are solely those of the author and do not necessarily reflect the views of the publisher, and the publisher hereby disclaims any responsibility for them.

DEDICATIONS

I want to dedicate this book to everyone who aspires to succeed in life and also to all those who have faced so much hindrances and obstacles in their lives and probably thinks that they can't succeed in the realization of their dreams and visions that is still in the inside of them. I want you to know that your obstacles and hindrances are only making a way for your victory and success and no doubt you will achieve success in your life. Congratulations in advance for your success.

ACKNOWLEDGEMENT

I want to give glory and praise to God for His continued inspiration upon my life to work on this very important project. I would also like to thank all my spiritual mentors whose lives and wisdom has tremendously enriched mine. I also want to acknowledge the ceaseless prayers of the ministers of House of Faith Mission and for their continued dedication to the ministry. May the good Lord continue to bless and keep you all in Jesus' name, amen.

ACKNOWLEDGMENTS

PREFACE

It is indeed important for us to understand that we are all born to succeed in life but regrettably though, not many people have really gone ahead to fulfil their heart's desires and purpose in their lives. God has put in the inside of every one everything we'll need to succeed in life, however if you don't realize it, you will continue to go round and round in a circle without actually making any headway at all. Your life is not meant to be wasted rather you are put here on earth to fulfil your purpose and assignment. Everything created in life is designed to solve a problem and nothing exists for nothing. Your eyes were made to see, your ears were made to hear and your hands were created to touch. When God created you He designed you to accomplish an assignment and if that assignment is not known, then one would be involved in all the wrong things and by so doing, one will be wasting one's precious time and purpose.

God as a matter of fact has deposited some dreams and visions in the inside of you that He wants you to accomplish and until you know this and begin to realize it in your life, your life will continue to remain unsettled and unstable. You need to understand that your dreams and visions are realizable and nothing in this life can stop you from accomplishing them if you are truly determined to succeed. God created you for success and failure is not your portion. Failure is not failure because one fails, no; its only failure if one remains in failure and refuses to try again.

You can be anything you want to be in life and you can achieve anything you set your heart to do. You can do all things through Christ who strengthens you. This book entitled, 'How to succeed in life' is written to motivate and inspire you to be victorious and successful in life. It is a book that would inspire and energize you to accomplish your dreams and visions.

It is true that sometimes when one has a dream and a vision one wants to achieve in life, there seems to be many obstacles and hindrances that tends to hinder one's progress, but we must not give in to them rather we should believe in God and in ourselves and go ahead and achieve our dream. Believing in oneself is very important if we are going to realize our dreams and visions. The only person that can stop you from achieving your dreams is no one else but you and if you refuse to be discouraged but move on to succeed in life, you will definitely succeed.

To really achieve success in life it actually begins with having a mind-set of success. It is what you perceive in your mind that you will achieve. As a man thinketh in his heart so is he. You cannot be negative in your thinking and then expect to achieve success. If you want success, then you need to see yourself succeeding and making your dreams and visions coming into manifestation and no doubt you will certainly see it come to pass.

Every dream or vision needs a lot of persistence and perseverance to see it materialize. We need to understand that we have all the resilience and ability to make it in life. Whatever you have in your heart to accomplish can certainly come to fruition if you continue to work towards it. In fact, one should not allow any ounce of discouragement to stop one from achieving one's goal. Once your mind is set to succeed you will no doubt succeed.

It is so pathetic that many have not truly discovered what their true purpose in life is and they have engaged themselves in endeavours that have continued to make them unhappy and frustrated. Your happiness and joy in life is determined by knowing and fulfilling your God ordained purpose and assignment. When you discover what your assignment is then you will live a life of fulfilment and your life will have meaning too.

God wants you to succeed and be all that He'd made you to be but there seems to be some contrary forces that tend to hinder this from happening. However, it is vitally important for you to know that you can succeed in life and your dreams can truly come into reality. Success is not the exclusive preserve of certain group of people rather it is for anyone who can believe in themselves and know in the inside of them that they can make it in life. Success is ahead of you and you have to be determined to strive towards it and embrace it into your life.

You need to know that whatever it is you want to see happen in your life is realizable and reachable. As you read this book you will be tremendously motivated to make it in your chosen field of endeavour and nothing will be able to stop you from moving forward or realizing your heart's desires. You have what it takes to succeed and if you will believe in yourself and work harder definitely you will no doubt succeed. You need to believe that with God all things are possible. Do not allow anything to limit you rather believe that you can achieve things for yourself. It is important for you to dream big dreams and stretch your mind to see things that looks impossible but trust God to see them come to pass. Whatever the magnitude of your dream or vision might be, just know that it can come to pass and it will surely come to pass.

My desire for you is that you will be everything that God has made you to be. Success is in the inside of you and you need to bring it out. You can make it and also know that nothing can stop you on your way to success. Success is just a step away from where you are right now and you need to take that step and don't allow anything to stop you or hinder you as you make your journey towards success.

CONTENTS

Dedications v
Acknowledgement vii
Preface ix

Chapter 1: Life is Meant To Be Lived................................... 1
    Life with meaning.. 3
    A life of purpose.. 5
    Knowing your assignment.. 6

Chapter 2: The Power Within 9
    Overcoming roadblocks 12
    Your motivation keeps you going 14
    Fear hinders success 15

Chapter 3: Walking In A Positive Mental Frame 17
    Overcoming negative thoughts 19
    The mind-set of winning 20

Chapter 4: If You Can See It, You Can Have It 22
    Abraham saw what God gave him.................................... 25

Chapter 5: The Power To Surmount Obstacles.................... 28
    Jehoshaphat in terrible situation 31
    The story of Hannah 33

Chapter 6: You Were Born To Succeed................................ 36
    The spirit of limitation... 40
    Limitations in our financial life 42

Chapter 7:   Hard Work Brings Success...44
   Acquiring excellence at what you do 47
   The spirit of a finisher...49

Chapter 8:   Reject Procrastination 51
   The spirit of commitment...53
   Focused energy 53

Chapter 9:   The I Can Philosophy..56
   Press on to obtain your dream...59

Chapter 10: Believe In God To Succeed 62
   Your trust in God 64
   Overcoming fiery trials...66

Chapter 11: Believe In Yourself 69
   Your spiritual power...72

Chapter 12: Take The Bull By The Horn..75
   The Lion's den 78

Chapter 13: Your Blessing Is Nearer Than You Thought..................81
   The sky is full of rain...84
   Rebellion blocks blessings 85

Chapter 14: The Power Of The Spoken Words 87
   Speaking to your dry bones..90

Chapter 15: Where There Is A Vision – Success Is Sure 92
   Running with your vision 96

Chapter 16: Breaking The Barrier Of Generational Curses 98
   Demons of limitations 101

Chapter 17: Having The Winning Attitude 104
   The joy of success 106
   Success makes life worth living...107

CHAPTER ONE

LIFE IS MEANT TO BE LIVED

"The thief cometh not, but for to steal, to kill, and to destroy: I am come that they might have life, and that they might have it more abundantly" (Jn. 10:10).

Life is given to us as a gift from God and it is meant to be enjoyed to the fullest. Many are merely existing and not living because they are living outside the will of God. God created life and He wants us to enjoy it and manifest His glory in the world. When life is lived outside of God, it becomes a drag and meaningless. One cannot fully understand life if he doesn't understand the giver of life. God is life Himself and when we know Him and have a relationship with Him, the mysteries of life becomes revealed unto us. Jesus made a statement, He said the thief has come to steal, kill and to destroy but I have come to give you life and life more abundantly (John 10:10). When we live outside of Christ's love, the devil begins to frustrate our lives and make it so meaningless that we become despondent and dissatisfied about it all.

A life without a vision and purpose leads to a life of non-achievement and setbacks. Life is meant to be lived purposefully and when one doesn't know his or her own purpose on earth, it leaves one hopeless and forlorn. When one has purpose in life, it gives one drive and motivation to achieve one's goals in life and which in turn gives one inspiration. Without inspiration in life, life becomes dull and mundane and that leads to the death of the soul. By death of the soul I mean that one becomes passionless and listless

Bishop Ben Ugbine

which is a sign of lethargy and it affects one's mind and when the mind is affected, it becomes a home for the devil and his demons to discourage one.

The mind of man is one of the greatest tools that God has given to mankind and when the mind is employed rightly, the result can be phenomenal. With the mind one can think thoughts that can revolutionize one's whole life. As a man thinketh in his heart so is he (Prov.23:7). Many people today are failures in life because of all the negative and destructive thoughts they have thought about themselves. If somebody thinks a thought of failure about themselves, pretty soon they will begin to experience it in their lives. Your thoughts shape your life and a good thought brings good result and bad thoughts bring bad result.

Your soul is a very vital part of you and what makes you to function properly and effectively in life is how well you can annex your mind with your emotions and also with your will. Your mind helps you to reason and process information and uses the information to regulate your life. The emotions of man are so vital because these are the seat of feelings and sensibility and it is from here one develops passion, drive, motivation, desire, love, anger and goodness. When the responses from the mind are healthy, the emotion picks up the equivalent responses and causes the person to have favourable emotional responses. On the other hand, the will of man puts all the reflexes received from the mind and emotions together and makes the consequent decisions which might be positive or negative. So we can see that the role of the soul is so important in helping one to live either a positive or a negative life depending on what is flowing from it. When the mind, the emotions and the will are not flowing the way the good Lord intended them to operate, it makes the life one lives here on earth to be deplorable. God wants us to be happy and successful in life but the keys to the mysteries of life are hidden in Him and when our ways are in consonant with His ways, we then experience what is called euphoria and our lives are full of excitement and meaning. God has the manual on how to operate life just as you have a manual on how to operate your VCR or any electronic gadget. When we operate life without the necessary manual, we find everything we encounter not working the way they should which can lead to hopelessness. The secret of life is in God so let's get acquainted with Him and He will unveil the hidden mysteries of life to us.

How to Succeed in Life

Life with meaning

A meaningful life is a blessed life. It is a life that is devoted to serving others and living sacrificially. Most people in life live a self-centred life and they are really not fulfilled and happy. When people are self-centred, they begin to think only of themselves and they lose out on the joy and fulfilment they should experience in serving others. It is very vital for us to give meaning to our lives and make it count and fulfilled. It is more blessed to give than to receive and sharing your gifts, talents, time, money and good with others will enhance the quality of your life. A selfish life is a life of misery and dejection and people whose sole life is to gratify themselves really do not feel satisfied and fulfilled.

It is important to understand that everything in life is meant to express itself out to others. The trees shed their leaves in order for them to receive new and fresh leaves. Can you imagine what will happen to a tree if it fails to shed its leaves? Of course we know that they will wither and die. Take the air we breathe for instance. We breathe in oxygen and give out carbon dioxide. Oxygen is released and it is used in the body and then it gives out the carbon dioxide and because of this exchange of give and take, man is able to survive.

Indeed, we can't over emphasize the importance of giving to God who Himself is a giver and He gave us everything including His only begotten son Jesus Christ. The gift of His Son today has caused us to be born again and come closer to Him. This one gift God gave has brought millions of souls unto Him.

When we share what we have with others, it causes God to make all grace abound towards us so that we can have all sufficiency in all things.

Indeed, the favour of God would always rest upon one when we are more altruistic and giving than when we are holding back.

In life seed time and harvest will not cease and whatever we sow is what will be multiplied back to us. Everything in life is a seed. Your time is a seed and your words are seeds. Even your smile or your kind gestures are

3

all seeds. When you give it, it will always be multiplied back to you in greater measure. Your love towards others is a seed and when you give love you will receive more love from others in return.

In all honesty, I believe that the greatest gift any man or woman can give to others is love and when we are living towards being a blessing to others we become tender, careful and more accommodating to people's weaknesses and idiosyncrasies. We are more careful in our actions in order not to hurt people's feelings. The word love is so all encompassing and broad in its application that if we really understand what it means then it will totally and completely change our whole approach to people and life.

We need to love one another and see how our lives can be of tremendous blessing to others and when we are walking in this divine love called Agape, then, we will become harmless and protected. But on the other hand, if we are not walking in love, we become fearful and afraid. **"Perfect love cast out all fears, for fear has torment"** (1 Jn. 4:18).

Walking in divine love is the motivating factor to every good intention in people's lives. People are more forgiving towards other people's short comings when they have love in their hearts. If I have the love of God ruling my life, then I will be quick to forgive other people's trespasses towards me and not hold grudges in my heart. Unforgiveness has caused many sorrows and diseases in people's lives because they would not forgive. When we fail to forgive others of their sins against us, the devil and his demons begins to use it to torment and afflict your life. These demons will cause your life to be depressed and without joy and also your body begins to age quickly and deteriorate.

A happy life is a life that is quick to forgive others of their mistakes and when we do that, God will also be quick to forgive us of our own mistakes too. Nobody is above mistakes and if we can be quick to forgive it will make our lives more joyful indeed. Walking in divine love is the key and when we give it generously, it will also cause us to receive favour from both God and man. What you sow is what you will reap.

A life of purpose

God wants us to live our lives purposefully and with a clear direction of where we are going. If you don't know where you are going, you will not know how to get there or when you arrive. Your life needs to have goals and definition and this will cause your life to have meaning, direction and clarity. If one knows where one is going, then one would map out the routes to one's destination and when the route is clear cut, then it is only a matter of time before one gets to one's destination. A purposeless life is an unfulfilled and wasted life. Your life is not meant to be wasted rather it is meant to be lived with great passion and joy and make it count in life. There is no such thing as a purposeless life rather people's lives become so because they have failed to discover who they are and what they are sent here on earth for. Our lives are designed to solve some problems which other people might have. For instance, my eyes were created to see and my ears were created to hear and my legs were created to walk. When everybody is able to discover their assignment and purpose in life, then their life becomes fulfilled and joyful.

For your life to be happy and meaningful, you need to discover what your assignment is in life. You need to discover the reason for God creating you and what problems you were sent here to solve. Until you know what problems you were sent here for, you will be doing all the wrong things in life and wasting your precious time and effort here on earth.

The saddest thing that can ever happen to a man is for him or her to live a life without knowing what their assignment is. You need to understand that your life is a gift and a blessing to somebody else but you need to discover what that is. Your doctor for instance solves medical problems, lawyers solve legal problems and of course your life is meant to solve a problem.

When we discover our purpose and what we are designed to do, life becomes meaningful and quite fulfilling. Your purpose is the reason for God creating you and that is what you were designed for. God in fact, put some special qualities in you that are uniquely suitable for your purpose and assignment. Your ability to sing, dance, play an instrument, talk or be generous to people are abilities and talents that are infused into you to effectively carry out your purpose.

The greatest tragedy that can ever happen to a man is for him to die without ever discovering his purpose. Indeed, many die without really knowing the reason for their being born into this world. It is vitally important for us to endeavour to know the reason why we are here. Have you ever heard the expression, 'Who am I?' The who am I is really referring to the reason for being born into this world and what work you were created for. If your assignment is to be a preacher or a teacher of the gospel, you will discover that your fulfilment and happiness will be generated when you are doing exactly that. If your purpose is to preach the gospel and you are working in the bank or doing something else for instance, you will not be satisfied even if you are paid a higher salary. Doing what you love most is a clue to your assignment and purpose. If for instance you love to design things, your purpose or your assignment might be a designer and if one puts one's total focus and effort towards it, then it could very well bring fulfilment and some financial reward as well.

Knowing your assignment

In life your assignment discovers you. By this I mean that when your assignment is known you become visible and productive and your life becomes useful to others. Many times your assignment brings you most of your financial reward and also gives you and others fulfilment and satisfaction that equally adds value and quality to your life. When your assignment is known, it causes you to be passionate over everything you do and your life is then filled with great enthusiasm. Frustration comes into people's lives because they are not doing what they love and they seem to be stocked with a job or work that tends to drain them of their energy and leaves them frustrated and depressed.

Life is too short to waste it on things one is not really passionate about and if we don't take 100% control of our lives today, then we will not truly achieve what we should achieve in life. You can actually turn your life

How to Succeed in Life

around today if you will endeavour to take absolute control of everything in your life. Nobody can really stop you from achieving your goals and dreams in life if one is really determined to make something tangible and real of their life. The only person that can truly stop you from achieving things is you and nobody else.

Success as they say starts in the mind and what you think you become. If you think success and do what is expected of you on a daily basis, success will come your way. Every road that leads to success starts with a thought or an idea and if this thought or idea is carried out with great passion and enthusiasm, it will become a reality. Your thoughts are seeds and if that seed is watered and fertilized in the womb of your mind, it will grow to become a tangible reality. We need to understand that dreams do come true if we hold on to them without wavering in our minds. Every achievement or success is determined by how much you allow that thought to overwhelm you to the point that nothing else matters to you except the fulfilment of that thought. Thoughts are powerful and they are the beginning process of every substantial achievement in life. In life you cannot rise more than your thoughts. If you think small thoughts that's what you will manifest and if you think big thoughts, no doubt you will manifest something big. The force or the gravity of your thought will determine what will be actualized into the physical manifestation. Great people have achieved great success in life because they chose to think great thoughts or dream big dreams.

The things you love to do are clues to your assignment and you must be positive in your mind that you can make something worthwhile with it.

When you discover what your assignment is then you need to develop it until you become so proficient at doing it. Mediocrity does not take one anywhere but people will honour and reward you for your excellence in what you do. Development and productivity is realized when one devotes one's effort and time into what they do and when it is done with great passion and interest, others begins to benefit from it as well. For instance, somebody who is interested in music will only succeed at it if he or she spends many hours a day perfecting that craft or skill. When one has attained to a reasonable level of excellence, then that gift or craft begins to bring them the desired reward or success. Success is a daily accomplishment that accumulates over a long period of time. There is no such thing as overnight success. Anything that is successful over-night usually doesn't last that long. For your success to be permanent and be forever rewarding, you have to make sure that it is something that has passed through the test of time. Many people have failed in life and become miserable because they were looking for over-night success or quick success. True success does not come to one that easily but one really has to work for it. This is the reason why those who win the lottery ends up being poor again because their success was not something they worked for rather it was thrust on them. When somebody achieves something they are not prepared for or trained for, that very thing could very well be the beginning of their trouble in life.

Your success will be permanent and rewarding when it becomes a pattern of a life style developed over the years and something that is done routinely. The things we enjoy doing on a daily basis could possibly be the very thing that brings success into our lives. We need to understand that success is a journey and not a destination. It is not a place you arrive at and then becomes complacent and fold your hands rather it is those things that you achieve on a daily basis. Success as a matter of fact should be progressive. In other words, it should be the different tasks and things we accomplish satisfactorily on a daily basis. When this is so in your life it brings a much more satisfactory experience into your life and your life becomes fulfilled and happy.

CHAPTER TWO

THE POWER WITHIN

"Behold, I give unto you power to thread on serpents and scorpions, and over all the power of the enemy: and nothing shall by any means hurt you" (Luke 10:19).

One of the biggest fallacies one can believe in one's life is to think that one cannot achieve one's dreams and goals in life. In fact, we have the power and ability to achieve success but regrettably, we have allowed people and circumstances to confuse our minds to think that our lives cannot amount to anything much. You can succeed in life if you think you can. The word can't and impossible are two words you must not allow in your vocabulary because they will limit you from achieving your goals and purposes in life. You can be anything you want to be and you can achieve anything you set your mind to achieve. People fail in life because they think failure and they believe that their dreams are unachievable. That is not correct because you have what it takes to succeed and success is in the inside of you.

The road to your success in life is determined by your mind-set and your daily confessions. What we say out of our mouth has a lot to do about what we experience in life. You can't think and speak negatively and expect something positive to happen to you. Your experience in life will be contingent upon the power of your words. Words are very powerful and they shape the subtotal of all of our lives experiences. If you really want to

Bishop Ben Ugbine

succeed in life, begin now to programme your mind with positive words that would energize and inspire you to achieve your goals and dreams.

Your success in life can be realized if you would daily learn to talk to yourself positively. You can say to yourself, **'I can make it and nothing can stop me in life, I would amount to greatness in my life'** and when you do this several times a day, your subconscious mind begins to believe it and work with it and it won't be long before you will begin to experience exactly what you've been confessing.

The power to succeed is within you and you just have to tap into it and make things happen for you. Your success in life is determined by you and nobody else. If you believe you can be a success you will. It all begins and ends with you. You know sometimes we are wont to think that the people who succeed in life are those who have come from a well to do families or are well educated and that is not really true. Anybody can succeed in life irrespective of their family background or educational standing. What makes people to succeed is what they believe about themselves and when you believe you can make, you will definetely make it. There have been stories of people with little or no education and poor family background who have made a name for themselves in life. Abraham Lincoln one of the greatest presidents America had ever had was from a poor background and he worked his way to success in spite of his limitations and setbacks.

When you endeavour to make it in life, obstacles would certainly set in to hinder you but you must not allow temporary situations to stop you from achieving your goals and dreams. In fact, true success does not really happen until one has faced many setbacks or many failures. Failure is not failure because you failed but you only become a failure when you completely give in and refuse to try again. Most people who have succeeded in life went through many failures but they used their failures as a springboard to their success. When we are persistent in life and refuse to give in to obstacles and failures or setbacks, success will greet us on the way. The problem with many people is that they give up too quickly and woefully refuse to put up a fight. To really succeed in life, you have to have a fighting spirit and make up in your mind that regardless of what you go

How to Succeed in Life

through in life or experience, you will not quit until you succeed. If you have this kind of mind-set or attitude, then be rest assured that you will be a success story.

When the vision of your dream is very clear to you no hindrance or obstacle in your way will stop you from moving forward. Your success and victory is ahead of you and not behind you. You must put every obstacles or evil events or occurrences in your life behind you and reach forth to what is ahead of you. Many times we allow circumstances or discouraging situations to blind our focus to where we are going and we lose sight of the vision ahead of us. No matter what you go through in life never you lose focus of your vision. Always put your vision before you so that temporary situations will not deter you from getting to your vision. If you lose focus of the vision, you know that your success and achievement will be hindered.

Focus is very vital in life to be able to achieve anything. Your obstacles and setbacks are designed for you to lose your focus so that your dream will not come to reality. You must fight that temptation to want to quit when things become tough or rough. You need to understand that every situation in life no matter the gravity of it is subject to change. No situation remains the same forever it will change if given some time. Many times you might be faced with situations and circumstances that might be so overwhelming, that your energy and enthusiasm begins to wane but that is the time to hold on and not quit nor give in. In such situations like this, you need to speak positive words to yourself to re-fire your motivation and passion. Words like, **'I am a winner and not a loser, greater is he that is in me than he that is in the world or I will not die but live and declare the works of the Lord,'** are statements or affirmations that will motivates you not to quit. Life is a fight and you must fight to stay alive and on top.

Many people in life have faced defeats and have given up on their dreams and goals because of obstacles that came their way and made them discouraged and disappointed. It is important to understand here that the border line between success and failure is so narrow that if people can understand this, they will try a little bit harder. In short it takes a little bit more effort at the point of failure to launch oneself to success. Failures are only a sign post to let you know that success is not very far from where you are. When people don't understand failure, then they think that it is a stop sign. It is not rather it is only showing us a new direction to take or go through.

We must not allow failure to stop us on our track to success rather we should endeavour to make new turns and move ahead. Your success to your dreams and goals are not far from you if you will not give up too soon but try a little bit harder.

In life you must expect to face some obstacles but be determined and resolute in your mind that nothing you face will stop you from achieving your dreams. Your dreams are realizable and they can become real if you can see it. What you see with your spiritual eyes, is what you can achieve if you can perceive it and hold on to it in your mind's eye, then before long, it will become an actuality and something tangible.

Overcoming roadblocks

Roadblocks are devices that are designed to quench and kill your effort on the road to your success. These roadblocks are there to tell you that your dreams cannot be achieved but you must not settle for that rather you must look for ways to overcome those roadblocks. In fact, this is where you draw on the power within you to empower you to move ahead. You must at this point programme your mind to think positively and not negatively. You need to tell your mind that this roadblock will not hinder you rather you will overcome it and move on to success. When these roadblocks come your way as they certainly will, speak to the roadblocks to give way and open an access door for you. As a man thinketh in his heart so is he (Prov. 23:7).

Roadblocks are temporary situations and when one is persistent and determined to move ahead, they will open opportunities for us to move ahead. Your roadblocks are opportunity for you to see the glory of God in your life. Until you face obstacles and situations you will not truly know how resilient and strong you are. God makes His grace available

How to Succeed in Life

to us in those moments when we feel vulnerable and incapable. The Apostle Paul experienced some road blocks in his life but hear what he said, **"For this thing I sought the Lord thrice, that it might depart from me. And he said unto me, 'My grace is sufficient for thee; for my strength is made perfect in weakness.' Most gladly therefore will I rather glory in my infirmities, that the power of Christ may rest upon me. Therefore, I take pleasure in infirmities, in reproaches, in necessities, in persecutions, in distresses for Christ's sake: for when I am weak, then am I strong"** (1 Cor. 12:8-10).

Don't give in too easily on your roadblocks but look for ways to overcome them. They are not the determining factors to your success rather it is your resolve and passion for your dreams that determines the result. You can really make it in life and your success is much closer to you than you even realize. Be determined to forge ahead in spite of what comes your way to oppose you. Winners don't quit and quitters don't win. You have to understand that you are a winner in the inside of you in spite of what the outside circumstances might reveal. We walk by faith and not by sight (1 Cor. 5:7).

If you only go by what you see physically you might become discouraged and give up on your dream. You must be able to see things with the eyes of faith and be determined to fight the good fight of faith. The good fight of faith is fought by constantly standing and confessing the word of God. What keeps you moving on in life in spite of circumstances and situations, is the word of faith you speak out of your mouth. Faith is what will bring your vision or dream into reality. The bible says that God calls the things that be not as though they were (Rom. 4:17b).

You need to call the things that be not as though they were. Speak as if your dream has already happened and you will see it happen. It's not a magic wand but it is the act of faith put into use. Faith begins with your confession and your confession forces the intangible things to be tangible. In other words, faith makes what is not seen to be seen. You have to see it first before you receive it and you have to believe it before you can handle, touch or see it

Your motivation keeps you going

The power within you can only be operated upon through your motivation. When a person is motivated to do something nothing they face in life can really stop them from making it. Motivation is the ability to run on to achieve something one has perceived intuitively and has had an inner fire or passion for that gives one the drive to move on. It is very hard and sometimes difficult to stop somebody from doing something they are truly and fully motivated about. Your motivation is the key to your success. If you are motivated nobody can talk you out of your dream or stop you from achieving it. One of the main reasons why people don't achieve success in what they try to do is because they are always waiting for somebody or someone to keep them energized. If you wait for people to energize you before doing any thing, your progress and achievement in life will be delayed and curtailed. For the most part you have to be your own self motivator by talking to yourself all the time. Many times people might not believe in you or in your dream and if you rely on them, you will be discouraged instead of being motivated. You should be your own cheer-leader and do everything it takes to always brace yourself up for your goals or dream. You may share your dream with somebody and they may say all kinds of things to try to discourage you but you must avoid such people on your path to success.

Once your motivation dies, your dream dies along with it. It is vital for you to surround yourself with positive people who will motivate you and not discourage you. Sometimes because of the size or level of your dream not many people will see things the way you see it. They may be seeing impossibilities whilst you are seeing possibilities and it is what you see and believe that God counts on.

Your motivation can also be fired up when you read books that inspires you to succeed. There are lots of books out there that can keep you motivated and achieve great things in your life. Certainly this book also should keep you motivated, read it over and over again and let the fire in you be ignited to usher you on to success or victory.

How to Succeed in Life

I want you to know that you can make it and it doesn't matter what you face or go through in life be rest assured that with God on your side, you can make things happen for you. You are the chief architect of your life and destiny and it is what you think of yourself you become. It is vitally important to have a mental frame of mind of success and success begins in your mind and what you think you become. Every victory or failure starts first in your mind. If you believe you can make it certainly you will make it.

You can turn your life around today if you will make a resolute decision to succeed in life. The journey of a thousand miles always begins with a step and you need to take that step today. Decide in your heart to succeed and you will succeed in whatever you want to accomplish in your life. You are the one that needs to make it happen and nobody else. When you make up your mind to succeed and achieve your dream, you will be amazed how everything will begin to line up in your life to bring your dream into reality. Things really happen when we take a step of faith. When you take the first step, God will align people in your life that would help facilitate the realization of your dream or vision. Favour comes to you when you take a step of faith and resist the temptation to walk in fear.

Fear hinders success

Fear is definitely the root cause of many people's failure in life. What they are afraid of comes upon them. Anything you are afraid of in life will certainly come upon you. If you are afraid of disease that fear will automatically cause it to happen to you. Fear is a spirit and it is a terrible demonic spirit that is designed to quench the fire in you to succeed and leave you hopeless and depressed. Fear and success doesn't go together. Anywhere you see fear be rest assured that you will see failure and lack of achievement.

To succeed in life, you must break the barrier and limitations of fear and know that with God on your side you can achieve what you want to achieve. Fear is simply false evidence appearing real. What you are afraid of is not real but mere illusions of the mind and it is a negative force to stop

Bishop Ben Ugbine

you on your track. Fear paralysis and it hinders one's progress in life. Your fear is the devil's power to frustrate and hinder you. Job made a statement thus, **"For my sighing cometh before I eat, and my roarings are poured out like the waters. For the things which I greatly feared is come upon me, and that which I was afraid of is come unto me. I was not in safety, neither had I rest, neither was I quiet; yet trouble came"** (Job 3:24-26).

What Job was afraid of came upon him. He was afraid of losing his children, his health and his wealth and he opened the door for the enemy to afflict him. The opposite of fear is faith and instead of entertaining fear, trust God and move by faith and get things done. Fear will not help you so resist the temptation to be afraid. Most times fear comes into our lives because of the unknown but you can turn your fears into faith and do it anyway. Feel the fear and do it anyway and see the power of God unveiled in your life and situation.

God has not given us the spirit of fear but of the power, of love and of sound mind (2 Tim. 1:7). Fear is from the enemy but faith and trust is from God. You see God knows that fear is a big problem for us that's why anytime He's going to use somebody He talks fear out of them. Lots of times when God wants to accomplish things with you or in your life the task will look so daunting that one would be scared to attempt it. Listen to what God said to Joshua when he was about to succeed Moses who died. **"Have not I commanded thee? Be strong and of a good courage; be not afraid, neither be thou dismayed; for the LORD thy God is with thee withersoever thou goest"** (Josh. 1:9).

Don't you ever be afraid just know that God is on your side and what He has put in your spirit He's able to bring it to pass. When fear tries to come into you, speak the fear out of you by speaking the word of faith. Faith word will cast out every fear that comes into you. Walk by faith and not by fear and you will accomplish great things in your life.

CHAPTER THREE

WALKING IN A POSITIVE MENTAL FRAME

"As a man thinketh in his heart so is he" (Prov. 23:7).

Your victory in life will certainly result from your mind - set. Being positive in life has a lot to do with our progress and when we think positive thoughts, things will no doubt change for us. With all the goings on in the world and all the razzmatazz of life, one can be tempted to be negative about what we think and feel about things. I do very well believe that a positive approach to life is the foundation to true success. Your positive mind-set has the generative power to turn things around in your favour. When we are pessimistic about things, they don't bring out a good outcome and this can also affect how we feel emotionally and psychologically.

The mind of man is one of the greatest assets that God has given to mankind and we can either use it in our favour or against oneself. Quite a great deal of people seems to have a defeatist mind-set and everything around them becomes confused and convoluted and they go through life disappointed and distraught. Your mind is your world and all the tapes and experiences of your life are recorded there and these tapes and experiences seem to affect how we view life. When somebody has had a bad experience in the past, they tend to project it into their now and it affects their perception about things and how they feel. Your mind controls your feelings. If you think sad experiences your feelings will interpret it and it will affect your mood and the way you behave. For instance, if you want to be happy, you have to start by thinking happy thoughts and that will be translated into your experience.

The mind of man is made up of the conscious and the unconscious. The conscious mind believes in reality and truth and it cannot be lied to or be deceived. If you say to the conscious mind that this picture is blue in colour when it is black and white, it will not believe it. It will only accept what is factual and real. On the other hand, the unconscious mind works on the direct opposite. It can be lied to and what is given to it is what it accepts. You can say to your unconscious mind that I am a millionaire and it will accept it and project that to you. For one to really succeed in life, that part of the mind needs to be employed positively to one's own advantage. You can programme positive thoughts and images into your unconscious mind and over a period of time, what you have programmed will begin to materialize.

In short, you can build an empire in your mind even before it is translated into paper and into materiality. You can build yourself a happy environment in your mind and see it affect your whole world. What you want your world to be will be based on your mental attitude and frame of mind. Your happiness and your peace of mind will be defined by what goes through your unconscious mind. Your mind is like your computer what you programmed into it is what it will display back to you. So if you are not feeling happy or peaceful in your life, then you need to begin to change the way you think. Your thinking can either mess your life up or make it productive and useful. It all depends on what flows in and out of your mind.

Every passing day millions of negative and positive thoughts floods through our minds but it's how you are able to control these thoughts that matters. Somebody can think a thought of murder and act on that thought and make their lives to become miserable and difficult whilst somebody else can think that same thought, but have the ability to control oneself. If we all act on all the thoughts that flood our minds daily, we will all be in serious trouble. We need to know what thought to act on and what to allow to go away. The way to overcome these negative thoughts is to let them flow in and out without acting on them but watch them like somebody standing by the sea side watching the waves move by without getting involved with it. Our actions give every thought the power and energy to be actualized. The ability to exercise self-control will play a greater role in controlling those negative thoughts that clouds our minds each day.

Overcoming negative thoughts

Thoughts shapes our lives and existence and they are the modulating factors for our sense of well-being and mannerisms and good thoughts brings good feelings and bad thoughts brings bad feelings. People's bad actions and attitude towards us many times can affect our feelings and they make us develop a negative mind-set towards them. In many instances, this negative mind-set leads to resentment and bitterness which begins to affect our health negatively. When you allow people's remarks to affect your mind, the enemy will use it to torment and cause you to be depressed and sad. Words are very powerful and when people say negative words to you they affect how you feel and react, and most times people don't react well because of the pain and the hurts they feel.

Many people have ended up in the hospital and mental institution very sick because of their negative approach and response to the negative words said to them. Indeed, bad words can really hurt but we have to protect ourselves by not giving in to bitterness and resentment which seem to fuel and aggravate the pain we feel inside.

The best way to overcome these negative destructive thoughts, is to always speak up our minds to people when they hurt us and let it go without allowing it to fester and give room to the enemy to torment us. Sometimes it is our reaction to what people say to us that really hurt rather than what was said. When we hear those negative words and let them roll off of us like water on a duck's back, then they will not do us any harm. You must protect yourself from people's negative words by restraining yourself from the temptation to hate. It is very important for us to be quick to forgive and let the love of God flow into our hearts. The love of God can dispel every evil word from messing up our minds to affect us.

Negative thoughts should be shielded from penetrating our lives by us regulating what we respond to. Our minds need to be renewed with the word of God so that only what God has decreed about us should penetrate us. Lots of times people are very cruel with their words and these words are demonically influenced to do us harm and if we are not vigilant and have total self-control, it will penetrate our minds to affect us.

It will take tremendous discipline not to fall into the temptation of responding to these words but if we can control ourselves, it will do us much good.

The mind-set of winning

To be victorious and successful in life we need to possess the mind-set of a winner and be able to hold that mind-set until we actually win. Often times those who become winners in their endeavours are those who are determined to make it. For instance, most athletes that win in their sport always picture themselves as winners even before they begin. When we focus on winning, we develop unusual inner strength and ability that tends to catapult us to victory.

Whatever it is you want to accomplish in your life, see yourself attaining it by having a mental picture of it actually happening. This is where visualization comes into play. Whatever you visualize in your mind's eye can truly be accomplished. Visualize yourself a winner or a success and pretty soon it will happen to you. Whatever you are involved in, see it already done even before you begin. You might be going through many trials and tribulations right now but see yourself coming out of it as a winner. Maybe your marriage is going through terrible affliction right now see yourself overcoming it and the situation will turn around. Most times when we are passing through terrible test and trials we tend to be hopeless and negative and don't believe that things can ever get better. Things can get better if we have a winning mind-set and let that mind-set override our situations. Whatever you picture in your mind in spite of the prevailing circumstances facing you, can really turn things around for the better.

We must not give up so easily but we must be determined to succeed and turn every situation or circumstance into something beautiful and good. Your mind is the power house for change and it is where your winning begins. You have to understand that you are already a winner even before you take the first step. Winning is not a destination but a positive mind-set that brings you to where you want to get to. The winning mind-set is like a driver of a car driving to a destination for him to get there, he has to see himself arriving at his destination even before he gets there. He may face many obstacles on the way but if he believes that he will get there, no doubt he will surely get there.

The winning mentality is very vital for your progress in life and it will see you through many setbacks and obstacles you might face in life. Once you know you are a winner, nothing you face or go through will ever stop you from achieving your heart's desires. God made you a winner and not a loser and winning was programmed into you by God. The bible says we are the express image of God and so if God is a winner in everything He does, then we are winners too. You have to know that it is impossible for you to fail and if you believe it no doubt it will work out well for you. You will face setbacks yes but that doesn't negate the fact that you are a winner. You are not only a winner but you are equally a champion and nothing you face can overcome you or defeat you. Every situation that comes across your way must bow before you. The power of God in the inside of you will annihilate every obstacle and hindrances the enemy will put on your way.

The demonic forces would always try to obstruct you reaching your destination but you must know that the greater One is in the inside of you and He will see you through the circumstances or situations you might even face in life. Your victory is guaranteed and you need to revel in it and appropriate it in your life. Don't allow your circumstances to determine who you are or where you can get to but be rest assured that God has already determined who you are and where you will get to.

Chapter Four

IF YOU CAN SEE IT, YOU CAN HAVE IT

"And the Lord said unto Abram, after that Lot was separated from him, lift up now thine eyes, and look from the place where thou art northward, and southward, and eastward, and westward: for all the land which thou seest, to thee will I give it, and to thy seed for ever. And I will make thy seed as the dust of the earth so that if a man can number the dust of the earth, then shall thy seed also be numbered. Arise, walk through the land in the length of it; for I will give it unto thee" (Gen. 13:14-17).

In life whatever we can perceive with our spiritual eyes we can possess. Everything that exists here in the physical realm had their original entity in the spiritual realm. For us to possess what God has given us we need to see it first with the eyes of the spirit before we can possess it in the natural. If you can see it, then it is yours. Most times the demonic forces tend to blind people's eyes so that they can't see the good things that the Lord has prepared for them from the foundation of the world. When people's eyes are not enlightened to see into the spirit realm, they begin to walk in limitations and lack. In the spiritual realm there is so much blessings laid out for us that if we can see them with our spiritual eyes, we will never suffer lack in our lives. We walk in lack and in limitations because we cannot see spiritually into the heaven-lies where there exists no lack whatsoever.

How to Succeed in Life

The word of God is clear concerning His blessings towards us. **"Blessed be the God and Father of our Lord Jesus Christ, who hath blessed us with all spiritual blessings in the heavenly places in Christ. According as he hath chosen us in him before the foundation of the world, that we should be holy and without blame before him in love"** (Eph. 1:3&4).

God had already blessed us even from the foundation of the world and everything we will ever need in our lives had already been taken care of even before we were born. All we have to do to walk in that blessing is to believe the word of God and let our spiritual eyes be enlightened to see these blessings. These blessings cannot be perceived with the mere physical eyes but it can only be perceived when our spiritual eyes are open to the spirit realm.

We need a revelative knowledge of what obtains and exists in the spiritual realm. The physical eyes can only perceive what it can see, feel and touch but the spiritual eyes have to see it first in the spiritual realm before it can even be felt physically. Spiritual things cannot be seen physically it can only be perceived spiritually. The Apostle Paul made this wonderful statement, **"That the God of our Lord Jesus Christ, the Father of glory, may give unto you the spirit of wisdom and revelation in the knowledge of him: the eyes of your understanding being enlightened, that ye may know what is the hope of his calling, and what the riches of the glory of his inheritance in the saints, and what is the exceeding greatness of his power to us-ward who believe, according to the working of his mighty power"** (Eph. 1:17-19).

We really need our spiritual eyes to be enlightened for us to perceive what we need to perceive in the spiritual realm. A blind person cannot physically see what is before him to possess. When we are spiritually blind we will continually be walking in ignorance of what God has given us and allow the forces of darkness to hinder our lives. God is a God of abundance and in the spiritual realm there are no limitations at all. Limitations and lack only exists here in the physical realm.

To possess what God has given you will require you to walk in the spirit before they can ever be perceived. Spiritual knowledge is very significant

Bishop Ben Ugbine

to receiving your God ordained blessings. **"My people perish for lack of knowledge"** (Hosea 4:6).

The knowledge of God's word is the fundamental key to receiving what is yours. If you don't know what God says in His word concerning you, you will be walking in ignorance and be denied your heavenly blessings. Knowledge is powerful and it is the reason for people's sufferings in life. Every problem that exists in human life is usually a problem of lack of knowledge. What you don't know is what is causing you to suffer the way you do. If you have the right knowledge concerning your situation, things will change for the better for you. One thing the devil doesn't want people to do is to walk in the true knowledge of God. He wants you to walk in ignorance and be hindered and suffer limitations in your life. **"In whom the god of this world hath blinded the minds of them which believe not, lest the light of the glorious gospel of Christ, who is the image of God should shine unto them"** (2 Cor. 4:4).

Walking in ignorance is the deadliest thing that can ever happen to a person because what you should see you cannot see. The reason why people cannot really see their blessings spiritually is because their minds have been so caught up with this physical life that they cannot see anything out of this life. We need to understand that the spiritual realm controls the physical realm and everything that exists here in the physical have their materiality in the spiritual realm. Your spiritual eyes need to be opened to see them so that you can possess what God says are yours. **"But as it is written, eyes hath not seen, nor ear heard, neither have entered into the heart of man, the things which God hath prepared for them that love him. But God hath revealed them unto us by his Spirit: for the Spirit searchest all things, yea, the deep things of God, for what man knoweth the things of a man, save the spirit of man which is in him? even so the things of God knoweth no man, but the Spirit of God"** (1 Cor. 2:9-11).

It takes the Spirit of God to know and perceive the things of the Spirit. Spiritual things cannot be comprehended with the carnal mind because they are not physical entities but spiritual. The carnal mind is completely

How to Succeed in Life

hostile to the things of God because it cannot understand them. **"For to be carnally minded is death; but to be spiritually minded is life and peace. Because the carnal mind is enmity against God, neither indeed can be, so then they that are in the flesh cannot please God"** (Rom. 8:6-8).

Walking in the Spirit of God will cause many wonderful blessings to flow into your life. God has blessed you with all spiritual blessings and you need to claim them for yourself. Don't allow ignorance or carnality to stop you from receiving what God says is yours. Walk by faith and possess what is yours and know that God has ordained it even from the foundation of the world for you to be blessed.

Abraham saw what God gave him

In Genesis chapter thirteen which we quoted at the beginning of this chapter God told Abram that He was going to bless him but that if he can see it then it is his. He told him that as far as he can see northward, southward, eastward and westward He has given to him. This is very vital because God can only give to you what you can see not only physically but also spiritually. Abram was distracted by Lot and his herdsmen who were fighting against Lots herdsmen and the land upon which they dwell could no longer contain them. Before God could bless him he had to separate himself from Lot his nephew because God cannot truly bless us when we are distracted. When he separated himself, God told him now you can look to every direction and whatever blessing you can see that I have given to you. In fact, God did not put any limitation as to what Abram could possess. Everything depended on what Abram could see before him. Abram knew that God had already blessed him because he knew that God's word will never return to Him void. But walking in the blessings of God would ultimately depend upon his vision of what he desired to possess.

Abram trusted God by faith and chose the land of Canaan and in that land God prospered and blessed him and that blessing is even flowing in our lives today as believers. The blessings of Abram or Abraham are upon us and we need to believe it and walk in it. God promised Abraham that

He was going to bless him and make him a father of many nations and that through him all the nations of the earth will be blessed (Gen 12:1-3).

The Abrahamic blessing is very significant in the lives of every believer because this is a covenant blessing that God made and we need to flow in that blessing. God is a covenant keeping God and whatever He says He will do He certainly will do it. **"My covenant will I not break, nor alter the things that is gone out of my lips"** (Psalm 89:34).

It is very significant and important that we lay hold to that Abrahamic blessing because that is the root source of our blessing as God spoke it to Abraham. **"Now the LORD had said unto Abram, Get thee out of thy Country, and from thy kindred, and from thy father's house, unto the land that I will shew thee: and I will make thee a great nation, and I will bless thee and make thy name great; and thou shalt be a blessing: and I will bless them that bless thee, and curse him that curseth thee, and in thee shall all the families of the earth be blessed"** (Gen. 12:1-3).

This blessing that God told Abram about was fully established as a covenant and God always deals with people by covenant. When a covenant is established it becomes binding for life and even one's children and great grand-children can inherit it from one generation to another. Through the Abrahamic covenant all Jews were blessed and those of us who are spiritual Jews or Israelites also partake of this great blessing.

We may have come from a cursed and poor family background but once we are washed by the blood of the Lamb, then we are no longer cursed but blessed. **"Christ hath redeemed us from the curse of the law, being made a curse for us; for it is written, cursed is every one that hangeth on a tree: that the blessing of Abraham might come on the Gentiles through Jesus Christ; that we might receive the promise of the Spirit through faith"** (Gal. 3:13&14).

Our spiritual eyes need to be opened to see what this blessing entails. If we can see it with our spiritual eyes, then we can receive it. Often times in our lives we tend to limit ourselves because of our prevailing circumstances and situations but we need to rise above that and be who God has already

How to Succeed in Life

declared us to be. If God says we are blessed, we better believe it and begin to claim the blessings into our lives.

When God calls us blessed He is not looking at our natural family background or circumstances rather He is going by His covenant that He made with Abraham who is a friend of God.

What do you see ahead of you? Can you see yourself already blessed in spite of where you are right now? Open your spiritual eyes and begin to see what God sees and walk in that blessing. If you cannot see the blessing, the devil will continue to hinder you and make you suffer lack when God has blessed you with His heavenly riches. When we talk about seeing this blessing, we are simply talking about having a discerning spirit as to what God has prepared for you. Before you came out of your mother's womb, your blessings had already been prepared and waiting for you to possess it. **"Before I formed thee in the belly I knew thee; and before thou camest forth out of the womb I sanctified thee, and I ordained thee a prophet unto the nations"** (Jer. 1:5).

Our spiritual sight needs to be enhanced so that we can see very clearly what God is doing and then flow with it. Most people miss out on God's blessings for them simply because they are walking outside of God's will and trying to figure out their lives by themselves. If we are God's children which we are, then it is right for us to let Him show us His plan and purpose for our lives. If we try to figure it out by our own self, we will be operating by trial and error and that might lead to a lot of conflict and sorrow in our lives.

It is basically what we can see of what God has planned for us that we can truly and surely possess. Open your spiritual eyes today and move from where you are now and possess everything that God says belongs to you. If you can see it, you can have it and no demon in hell can stop you from receiving what God has given to you even from the foundation of the world.

Chapter Five

THE POWER TO SURMOUNT OBSTACLES

"I will lift up mine eyes unto the hills, from whence cometh my help. My help cometh from the LORD, which made the heavens and the earth" (Psalm 121:1&2).

Life indeed is full of ups and downs and we all go through many difficult situations in our lives that sometimes seem unbearable. Some of these problems are sometimes so overwhelming that it leaves us emotionally drained and physically destroyed. Life itself is tough and it takes a tough minded person to survive without ending up in a mental home or in the hospital. Many of these problems and troubles that come upon one most times appear unbearable so much so that often times one just wants to end it all up. We need to understand that tough times don't last only tough people do. No matter how overwhelming your problem or situation might be, you need to know that you can overcome them and be triumphant. You will not die but live and you will put the devil and all your adversaries to shame.

"Many are the afflictions of the righteous; but the LORD delivereth him out of them all. He keepeth all his bones: not one of them is broken" (Psalm 34:19).

How to Succeed in Life

God is the strength of your life and He will never allow the enemy to destroy you. His covering is over you and He will enlist His holy angels to fight on your behalf and you can be sure that the victory will be yours. When we are faced with life's battles and situations, we need to know that the battle is the Lord's and He will fight it for us and give us victory. When we fight a battle that only God should fight for us, we make a mess of it and cause more harm and sorrow upon our lives but if God assumes your battle, be rest assured that the victory will be sweet.

When people are fighting you just commit them to the Lord and let Him take absolute control of the situation. Sometimes the troubles we face makes us so fearful and confused that for the most part we feel like giving up but you must not give up. Hold on to God and let Him deliver you. **"And call upon me in the day of trouble; I will deliver thee, and thou shalt glorify me"** (Psalm 50:15).

God wants us to call upon Him when we are troubled and He truly wants to help us to overcome. When we are faced with turbulent situations, we must resist the temptation to run helter-skelter to people for help. We need to go before the Lord so that He can help us by showing us a way to overcome the situation. God is the only one that can truly help us and deliver us from every power of the wicked one. The Apostle Paul was a man that was faced with many troubles but he trusted in God and God delivered him from the hands of his enemies**. "We are troubled on every side, yet not distressed; we are perplexed, but not in despair; persecuted, but not destroyed; always bearing about in the body the dying of the Lord Jesus, that the life also of Jesus might be made manifest in our body"** (2 Cor. 4:810).

When we are troubled, we should realize that the angels of God are encamping around us and they will not leave us forsaken. **"For he shall give his angels charge over thee, to keep thee in all thy ways. They shall bear thee up in their hands, lest thou dash thy foot against a stone"** (Psalm 91:11&12). God's protection over you is a very sure thing and you have to believe that God is much closer to you than your breath. He will never leave you nor forsake you (Hebs 13:5). When you walk in

Bishop Ben Ugbine

the darkest moments of your life He will be with you to shield you. **"Yea, though I walk through the valley of the shadow of death, I will fear no evil: for thou art with me; thy rod and thy staff they comfort me"** (Psalm 23:4).

The valley of the shadow of death will not overwhelm you and of course God will be present to deliver you. In life, we will walk through situations that really seems so life threatening and many times it may appear like we are not going to come out of it but let me reassure you that the greater your trials and afflictions, the more God is ready to deliver you. When the enemy comes with all his ferocious attacks, God will match his own forces against him and he will be defeated. **"So shall they fear the name of the LORD from the West, and his glory from the rising of the sun. When the enemy shall come in like the flood, the Spirit of the LORD shall lift up a standard against him"** (Isaiah 59:19).

God's angelic forces is surely greater than the forces of all your adversaries and be certain that the victory will be yours. Nobody touches a child of the living God and not see the wrath of God in manifestation. Vengeance belongs to God and allow Him to give you sweet justice. God is never asleep and He knows every trials and situations and obstacles we are faced with and He will be there to help us. Don't be afraid of the number of people that are fighting against you God will keep you from every harm. **"A thousand shall fall at thy side, and ten thousand at thy right hand; but it shall not come nigh thee. Only with thine eyes shall thou behold and see the reward of the wicked"** (Psalm 91:7&8).

I want you to realize that there are more with you than are with your enemies. Your enemy might look stronger and powerful but God would always bring them down with His mighty power. When Goliath came against David to destroy him, David depended on his God and God gave him victory over Goliath. Goliath came against David with spear and sword but David went against him in the name of the Lord and brought the mighty Goliath down just with a sling and a stone. **"Then David said to the Philistine, Thou comest to me with a sword, and with a spear, and with a shield: but I come to thee in the name of the LORD of**

How to Succeed in Life

hosts, the God of the armies of Israel, whom thou hast defied. This day will the LORD deliver thee into mine hand; and I will smite thee, and take thine head from thee; and I will give the carcases of the host of the Philistines this day to the wild beasts of the earth; that all the earth may know that there is a God in Israel. And all this assembly shall know that the Lord saveth not with sword and spear: for the battle is the LORD's, and he will give you into our hands" (1 Sam. 17:45-47). And in the next few verses it shows David's victory over Goliath. "And David put his hand in his bag, and took thence a stone, and a sling, and smote the Philistine in his forehead that the stone sunk into his forehead; and he fell upon his face to the earth. So David prevailed over the Philistine with a sling and with a stone, and smote the Philistine, and slew him: but there was no sword in the hand of David. Therefore, David ran, and stood upon the Philistine, and took his shealth thereof, and slew him, and cut off his head therewith. And when the Philistines saw their champion death, they fled" (1 Sam. 17:49-51).

David gained victory over Goliath because he relied on God and not on the arm of flesh. Most times we want to rely on the arm of flesh and do what we feel like doing. We don't have to fight the battle ourselves but we allow God to fight the battle and God knows our enemies better than you know them and He knows the best method to use to bring your enemy down.

Jehoshaphat in terrible situation
(2 Chron. 20:1-25)

The story of Jehoshaphat is a classic example of how God can show His delivering power on those who trust in Him for help. Jehoshaphat was faced with a terrible problem because the Moabites, Ammonites and Mount Seir gathered together to come against the tribe of Judah. They wanted to completely destroy the tribe of Judah and Jehoshaphat and the people cried unto God for help and He came to their rescue. "It came to pass after this also, that the children of Moab and the children of Ammon, and with them other besides the Ammonites, came against Jehoshaphat to battle. Then there came some that told Jehoshaphat, saying, There cometh a great multitude against thee from beyond the sea on this side of Syria; and, behold, they be in Hazazon-tamar, which is Engedi. And Jehoshaphat feared and set himself to seek the LORD, and proclaimed a fast throughout all Judah" (2 Chron. 20:1-3).

Jehoshaphat was really afraid of the great force that was coming against them and solicited the help of the Lord. Indeed, the Lord gave him a plan and told him to use the weapon of praise to fight the battle. He instructed the people and they took their trumpet and began to praise the name of the Lord and the Lord caused confusion in the camp of their enemies and they all began to fight against themselves until they destroyed one another. As a matter of fact, when Jehoshaphat and his people woke up the next morning, all their enemies were dead without them even lifting up a finger. That's exactly what will happen to all of our adversaries when we allow the Lord to fight the battle for us. The battle belongs to the Lord and He will surely give us the victory.

Jehoshaphat and his people were left with abundance of blessings which was so much that it took them three whole days to collect all the blessings. "And when Jehoshaphat and his people came to take away the spoil of them, they found among them in abundance both riches with the dead bodies, and precious jewels, which they stripped off for themselves, more than they could carry away: and they were three days in gathering of the spoil, it was so much" (2 Chron. 20:25).

Anytime the devil and his forces come against you with an overwhelming force, they are only making way for a great blessing for you. Sometimes when God really wants to bless you in a mighty way, He schedules the enemy to attack you for His glory to be revealed in your life. Every attack you see coming into your life that appears terrifying just see it as your opportunity to be blessed in a big way. There is something about the anointing power of God in your life it sometimes attracts trouble. The anointing of God in your life can only be increased when you have overcome the ferocious attacks of the enemy. The attacks of the enemy are really an opportunity for your blessings to be revealed.

How to Succeed in Life

Don't be scared when trouble comes your way but just stand still and see the salvation of the Lord in your life. God is your helper and He will be there to deliver you from the hands of the evil one. Even when you feel terrified and panicky, just calm yourself down and know that God's great army is ready and willing to do battle for you.

The story of Hannah
(1 Sam. 1&2)

Hannah went through some harrowing experiences with her mate because she was barren and her mate Penninah had children. Because of her barrenness, Penninah tormented her sore and made her life unbearable to the point that out of frustration and sorrow she cried unto the Lord for help. When a woman is married and unable to conceive, it's indeed a terrible situation for her especially in a culture where such condition is heavily despised. For a woman to be married and not have a child is almost like she doesn't exist at all. It is even worse when that woman is in a polygamous family where her mates could really make her feel severely miserable. **"Now there was a certain man of Ra-matha-im-zo-phin, of Mount Ephr-im and his name was El-kanah, the son of Jeroham, the son of Elihu, the son of Johu, the son of Zuph, an Ephrathite: and he had two wives; and the name of the one was Hannah, and the name of the other Penninah: and Penninah had children, but Hannah had no children. And this man went up out of his city yearly to worship and to sacrifice unto the LORD of hosts in Shiloh. And the two sons of Eli, Hophni and Phinehas, the priest of the LORD, were there. And when the times was that Elkanah offered, he gave to Penninah his wife, and to all her sons and her daughters, portion: but unto Hannah he gave a worthy portion; for he loved Hannah: but the LORD had shut her womb. And her adversary also provoked her sore, for to make her fret, because the LORD had shut her womb. And as he did so year by year, when she went up to the house of the LORD, so she provoked her; therefore, she wept and did not eat"** (1 Sam. 1:1-7).

Hannah took her pain and sorrow to the Lord and she poured her heart unto God for help and indeed God heard her cry and affliction and opened up her womb and she conceived. Hannah made a vow to God that if He would give her a male child she would offer him back to God to serve in His house all the days of his life. In short, God hearkened unto her petition and she gave birth to Prophet Samuel who became a great prophet in Israel. She allowed God to fight her battle and God brought joy and happiness back into her life. Penninah and her children that made Hannah sorrowful were made to be ashamed of their reproach of her. In fact, the Lord blessed Hannah with more children when she gave back Samuel unto the Lord. **"And the LORD visited Hannah, so that she conceived, and bare three sons and two daughters. And the child Samuel grew before the LORD"** (1 Sam. 2:21).

Many are the afflictions of the righteous but the Lord will see him through them all. God knows every problem we go through even before we go through them and He will always make a way of escape for us. Your temptations and trials are only making way for your greatness. What you are going through right now, you will overcome them and glorify God.

You will not drown in your problem and afflictions but God would keep you so that you will not be harmed or hurt by it. **"When thou passeth through the waters, I will be with thee: and through the rivers, they shall not overflow thee: when thou walkest through the fire, thou shalt not be burned; neither shall the flame kindle upon thee"** (Isaiah 43:2).

God has already made a way of escape for you and He has also given you the grace to go through what you are going through right now and come out on the other side tremendously blessed. **"There hath no temptation taken you but such as is common to man: but God is faithful, who will not suffer you to be tempted above that ye are able; but will with the temptation also make a way of escape, that ye may be able to bear it"** (1 Cor. 10:13).

Every situation you are currently going through is not above your capacity to handle. God knows that you are well able to handle it hence he allowed it to come your way and He will use this very trial to beautify your life and make you rejoice at the other side of the trials.

How to Succeed in Life

There is always the other side of every trial and when you arrive at the other side, you will be greeted with joy and abundance of blessing. Child of God, I want you to rejoice and praise God even in the midst of your terrible trials and afflictions because there is a great celebration of victory and tremendous blessing awaiting you to receive. Sheer up God indeed is on your side and you will not drown and you cannot fail either. Victory is on your side and deliverance is also on your side and God's grace will certainly see you through and all your adversities which are only temporary will certainly pass away.

CHAPTER SIX

YOU WERE BORN TO SUCCEED

"Now thanks be unto God, which always causeth us to triumph in Christ, and maketh manifest the savour of his knowledge by us in every place" (2 Cor. 2:14).

One thing we must allow to register very clearly in our minds as we go about our daily routine and responsibilities, is that we are born to succeed. If this fact is rooted in your mind, you will always move from one accomplishment to another. When you partnership with God, He will energize and cause you to make it in whatever you do. One of the things that makes people not to succeed in their chosen endeavours is that they are basing their success on their own strength and ability. When you take on the ability and strength of God to do what you plan to do, He would cause you to achieve tremendous success far beyond your wildest dreams. God's divine ability and enablement is what you need to make you ride high in life. With our own human abilities, we are limited but with God's power upon us, we become limitless and unconquerable.

God's dunamis power which is the inherent and active power of God will turn us from mere human being to a supernatural being operating in the divine dimension of God. The word power in Greek has different meanings. There are four specific words used to describe the different operative power of God. You have dunamis, energia, cratos and Iscius and I will explain their different meanings so that you can be clear concerning this power of

How to Succeed in Life

God. Dunamis as explained above is the inherent and active power of God that He has in Him. The energia power of God is simply God's power in exercise – in other words this is the working power of God that transmits this force of God unto us. The cratos power of God is His manifested power as seen in operation and then of course the Iscius power of God is the power endowed or received in us. The dunamis power of God is carried by energia and manifested by cratos and then endowed by the Iscius power of God. And this power flows in us and it's to be used or put into operation by the energia power of God. The exousia power of God is simply the authority God has given us to decree things and to bring things into manifestation. God wants us to know that we have His power in us and He wants us to use the power with authority. If we are going to succeed in life and in our walk with God, we need to understand our authority in Him and use it effectively.

One of the reasons why we don't seem to see things happen in our lives the way we should is because we have failed to exercise the power and authority we have in the name of Jesus. **"Behold, I give unto you power to tread on serpents and scorpions, and over all the power of the enemy: and nothing shall any means hurt you"** (Luke 10:19).

The name of Jesus is above every other name and it is in this name that we have victory. Whatever force that seems to come against you the name of Jesus will over power them. **"Wherefore God also hath highly exalted him, and given him a name which is above every name: that at the name of Jesus every knee should bow, of things in heaven, and things in earth, and things under the earth; and that every tongue should confess that Jesus Christ is Lord, to the glory of God the Father"** (Phil. 2:9-11).

The name of Jesus is above failure, poverty, sickness, fear, setbacks, limitations, anger, mental problems and it is also above any name that can ever be mentioned. We need to exercise our authority and command every forces of darkness that rises up against us to stop. Whatever you say out of your mouth, God must honour it and as a result we need to speak with boldness. **"Verily I say unto you, whatever ye shall bind on earth shall be bound in heaven: and whatsoever ye shall loose on earth shall be loosed in heaven"** (Matt. 18:18).

Bishop Ben Ugbine

You possess the power to bind all the demonic forces that seems to be working against you not to progress in life. If you don't succeed, it is not because God doesn't want you to but it is simply because you have failed to use and exercise your authority in Christ. Certainly the forces of darkness will most times rise up against you but you have to be confident that the gates of hell shall not prevail against you. God did not say that you will not go through problems but He expects you not to give in and lose your faith in spite of what you face in life. One of the things the devil and his forces are really after in your life is your faith. If he can destroy your faith, he has succeeded in destroying your success and accomplishments. Jesus told Peter not to lose his faith as he goes through his harrowing trials and experiences with the devil. **"And the Lord said, Simon, Simon, behold, Satan hath desired to have, that he may sift you as wheat: but I have prayed for thee, that thy faith fail not: and when thou art converted, strengthen thy brethren"** (Luke 22:31&32).

Jesus knew that Satan was going to tempt Peter and that he was going to deny the Lord but the Lord assured him that because He had chosen him and has also prayed for him, he should not allow his faith to fail. Trials and situations will certainly come our way but we must hang in there and trust in God and never give up hope on our deliverance.

Certainly the devil almost derailed Peter's faith because he wanted to abort Peter's destiny but thank God Peter repented of his denial against Jesus and became a mighty instrument in establishing the early church and also in the hand of God. No matter what oppositions you are currently passing through right now, be rest assured that your faith will not fail and the gates of hell will not prevail against you. Certainly they will come against you, but they will not prevail against you because God is on your side and you are built upon a solid rock – which is Christ. **"And I say also unto thee, That thou art Peter, and upon this rock I will build my church; and the gates of hell shall not prevail against it"** (Matt. 16:18).

The gates of hell represent the demonic forces and their job is to steal, to kill and to destroy but Jesus has come to give us abundant life. **"The thief cometh not, but for to steal, and to kill, and to destroy: I am come that**

How to Succeed in Life

they might have life, and that they might have it more abundantly" (John 10:10).

Abundant life is yours and God wants you to have it in every area of your life. The devil has no right or authority to temper with what God says is yours and you need to believe that and act upon it. This abundant life is not what you are going to have rather it is what you possess right now. God always blesses in the now and not tomorrow. His blessings have already been established from the foundation of the world and they exist right now in your life. His blessings have already been decreed and we need to walk in them. **"And all these blessings shall come on thee, and overtake thee, if thou shalt hearken unto the voice of the LORD thy God. Blessed shall thou be in the City, and blessed shalt thou be in the field. Blessed shall be the fruit of thy body and the fruit of thy ground, and the fruit of thy cattle, the increase of thy kine, and the flocks of thy sheep. Blessed shall be thy basket and thy store. Blessed shalt thou be when thou comest in and blessed shalt thou be when thou goest out. The LORD shall cause thine enemies that rise up against thee to be smitten before thy face: they shall come out against thee one way, and flee before thee seven ways. The LORD shall command the blessing upon thee in thy storehouses, and in all that thou setest thine hand unto; and he shall bless thee in the land which the LORD thy God giveth thee"** (Deut 28:2-8).

All the blessings God mentioned above is meant for us to succeed and we need to appropriate them into our lives. He said He will bless the work of our hands which means that you have to be doing something for God to bless. God cannot bless nothing and He only blesses what you are legitimately doing and He has promised to prosper it. If God says He will prosper you of course you know it is a done deal. Let your hand find something you love to do and put your hundred percent attention to it and God would bless it. Success is yours but you have to work for it. It will not fall on your lap so easily like that because spiritual principles demand that what you sow is what you will reap. If you sow hard work and diligence in what you do, you will see God bless it.

Bishop Ben Ugbine

The spirit of limitation

The spirit of limitation is a deadly spirit and it's the spirit that causes stagnation to come upon your life. Once you are limited in your life, you will be living a depressed and suppressed life and whatever you do will not amount to much. When the spirit of limitation is upon you, you will be putting more energy and effort but the reward you receive will be less compared to the effort you've put in. Limitation leads to frustration and it could even lead to people committing suicide because they often consider themselves as failures in life.

The demonic forces have succeeded in limiting countless people in their lives so much so that many have become disappointed, discouraged and disillusioned about life. When your life is limited, opportunities will always pass you by and struggle will be a part of what you continue to experience. If you are limited and you are in business, the business would never exceed certain level. In fact, the business will be going up and down and will never pass a level for you to experience progress. And this in short can cause terrible depression and make you look like you are a failure in life.

Many people today are living a life of limitation in their marriages, in their ministries, in their jobs and even in their physical health. One area that the devil fights people a lot is withthe spirit of limitation in the area of their marriage. The devil hates the power of two and he hates two people coming together in agreement to do something and he would do anything to limit them. Many marriages are being frustrated and broken because the marriage cannot seem to pass a certain level of progress or success. When people are limited in their marriage, they would quarrel and fight over little things that don't even matter much. Limitation in marriage causes spouses to work against themselves and not agree on anything. In fact, the love level in the marriage is brought to a low level that many times the marriage breaks up and result in divorce.

Your marriage is given to you by God to enjoy and support and encourage one another to succeed. Both partners in a marriage should work together to see to the progress of each other and not fight against each other. The devil wants couples to fight and not be in agreement and then live in

How to Succeed in Life

limitation and in frustration. There is nothing so frustrating and limiting in life when couples don't agree with each other.

When people don't agree together, it is practically impossible for them to achieve the success they are supposed to achieve. Agreement is a powerful thing and if people can understand the power of two then nothing in life can really stop them from succeeding. Two people in agreement can achieve much more than they can achieve on their own. **"Again I say unto you, That if two of you shall agree on earth as touching anything that they shall ask, it shall be done for them"** (Matt. 18:19).

For two people to walk together, they have to agree otherwise the devil will limit them and all their effort together will be frustrated. **"Can two walk together; except they be agreed?"** (Amos 3:3).

To overcome limitations in your life, you need to walk in obedience in God's word. A lot of times people experience limitation in their lives because of their rebellion and disobedience to the word of God. When we walk in rebellion then a door is opened for the devil to afflict us and limit us in what we should accomplish. Obedience is a very big key to breaking the spirit of limitation in our lives. When a wife rebels against her husband, then her life becomes limited and frustrated. Today many wives are walking in rebellion and in disobedience and they want to take control of the home and that is not the right order of God. God expects the woman to be submissive to the husband and the husband is commanded to love and cherish his wife. When the wife submits and the husband loves his wife, then the spirit of progress will be released upon them and the devil cannot limit them.

We need to stand on the word of God concerning marriage and do what God has commanded us to do. The wife must not withhold sex from her husband otherwise she would open the door for the adversary to hinder and limit God's joy in the marriage. I strongly believe that people can experience joy in their marriage if they would walk in obedience and in wisdom. Wisdom is a key thing in having a good marriage. Most problems we have in our lives are rooted in lack of knowledge or in ignorance. What you don't know can hinder and limit your life. **"My people perish for**

lack of knowledge" (Hosea 4:6). When we have proper and accurate knowledge of how to relate with ourselves then life becomes sweet and easy. The knowledge of God gives us the divine wisdom to apply knowledge correctly. Walk in wisdom and you will break the spirit of limitation from your life. **"Wisdom is the principal thing; therefore get wisdom: and with all thy getting get understanding"** (Prov. 4:7).

When we walk in God's wisdom His favour comes into our lives and we are able to succeed in what we do. The wisdom of God would help us in every area of our lives be it financial, physical or spiritual. Wisdom is the ability to apply knowledge correctly or the ability to discern difference in people, places and things. When people walk in foolishness and ignorance, it causes their lives to go through many troubles and limitations.

God has blessed you and you need to walk in obedience so that you can eat the good of the land. Rebellion is a demonic spirit and it is designed to limit your life from enjoying the fullness of God's blessings upon your life. **"If you be willing and obedient, ye shall eat the good of the land: but if ye refuse and rebel, ye shall be devoured with the sword: for the mouth of the LORD hath spoken it"** (Isaiah 1:19&20).

Limitation is not your portion and God wants you to soar like the eagle and be successful in life. Let God's word be rooted and grounded in you and nothing will be able to stop you from achieving what you set your heart to do. In every area of your life, let God's word have a strong hold of it and be quick to obey God's word in your life and His favour will come upon you to succeed and you will be fully blessed and successful.

Limitations in our financial life

This is probably one of the greatest areas that many have been hindered and limited by the forces of darkness. Money plays a lot of role in our lives and when we don't have enough of it, it affects what we are able to achieve or accomplish in life. Many, today are walking in financial limitations because they have failed to follow God's laid down principles concerning financial prosperity. When we don't give to God what belongs to Him, then the devourers are released to attack our finances and we experience total lack in our lives. God expects us to pay our tithe and give Him what belongs to Him. Ten percent of what we earn belongs to Him and if we give it to Him, He would cause His blessings to flow into our lives. One cannot be blessed financially when we withhold God's money. If we really want to walk in financial supply, we must be obedient to the law of tithing. **"Will a man rob God? Yet ye have robbed me. But ye say, Wherein have we robbed thee? In tithe and offerings. Ye are cursed with a curse: for ye have robbed me, even this whole nation. Bring ye all the tithes into the storehouse, that there may be meat in mine house, and prove me now herewith, saith the LORD of hosts, If I will not open you the windows of heaven, and pour you out a blessing, that there shall not be room enough to receive it. And I will rebuke the devourers for your sakes, and he shall not destroy the fruit of your ground; neither shall your vine cast her fruit before the time in the field, saith the LORD of hosts"** (Mal. 3:8-11).

The secret of walking in God's abundance is to be obedient to tithing and sowing seed into the work of God. Sowing and reaping is a supernatural law that works in every facets of our life. Whatever we sow comes back to us in greater measure. Your blessings cannot flow effectively if you are not sowing anything. If you sow nothing you will receive nothing in return. People want financial blessings upon their lives but they don't want to pay their tithes nor sow any seed to the things of God. When we fail to operate in this law of sowing and reaping, the devourers begins to plague our financial life and we continue to suffer financial limitations.

Walk in obedience to this law of sowing and reaping and see what happens in your life. When you hold back what you should release as your seed, you will not receive a harvest. Your harvest is depended upon your seed that you release. Supply will always respond to sowing. When a farmer wants a harvest he sows seeds and with time he reaps a great harvest.

Start today to be a tither and a giver and you will never suffer financial limitations in your life again. You are not supposed to suffer lack because God has blessed us with all spiritual things in the heavenly places and you need to follow His spiritual laws of financial blessings to prosper.

CHAPTER SEVEN

HARD WORK BRINGS SUCCESS

"Seest thou a man diligent in his business? He shall stand before kings; he shall not stand before mean men" (Prov. 22:29).

Hard work is the secret to great success. Idleness and indolence leads to poverty and lack and for you to forge ahead and make it, you have to put your hand on the plough and not look back. Hard work requires dedication and commitment to one's work and that would guarantee one great reward. Laziness is the twin brother of poverty and a lazy person cannot enjoy the fullness of life because they would constantly be in want. God expects us to work with our hands and make a living for ourselves. He does not expect us to be indolent and continue to live off on other people. When you begin to depend on people to take care of you, when you should do that for yourself, you lose your sense of dignity and self-respect. People will continue to despise you when they know that you are depending on them to cater for you and sustain you. Anyone that provides for you when you are well able to provide for yourself, will ultimately control your life and you will never be happy. It is important that you make something out for yourself so that you can buy what you need instead of struggling to survive all through your life.

In our society today, people value and respect you by what you do. Your work or job defines how people will categorize and honour you. Your work or job is what should provide you the resources or the money you need to cater for yourself and your family as the case may be, if you do have a family.

How to Succeed in Life

For one to aspire to make it in life, it definitely requires great diligence and dedication on one's part. Nothing will amount to much if a lot of effort is not put into it. When we work hard to achieve something, God would certainly show us His favour so that we can achieve good result. An athlete who wants to achieve success had to spend hours upon hours to train in his or her field in order to win. Even a boxer who wants to win a fight trains daily for months to be ready for the fight. It is ridiculous for a boxer to wake up one morning and decides he wants to fight the next day without adequate preparation. Of course without being told we know that he would suffer a terrible defeat if he attempts it. Those who want to achieve success without much preparation, would only be greeted with disappointment and shame. Anything worthwhile in life requires time to come to full maturation and we can't run away from that fact.

A diligent man would be rewarded with much wealth and abundance and he would equally gain the respect and admiration of others around him. Your success in life will be depended upon how bad you really want it. If it's something that means a world to you and you want to spend the rest of your life doing it, then you must pour yourself into it and work at it day and night. Whatever you pour yourself into, no doubt it will bring you success. Indeed, your success in what you do will depend on how much you have mastered it and what you have mastered will ultimately bring pleasure to others and equally bring you monetary reward as well. Your hard work and dedication to your calling or dreams and visions is never in vain because given the right and appropriate time, it will yield you tremendous fruit and reward. The benefits of hard work cannot be over emphasized because it is the bed rock of great achievements in life.

Hard work requires a lot of sacrifice and focus and we need to focus on what matters a lot to you and then your attention will be minimized on less important things. When your attention is focused on your goals and dreams or occupation as the case may be, then you become totally blind to other insignificant things. You cannot achieve great success in life when you are involved with many things at the same time. Your expertise and professionalism will be discovered when you give yourself wholly to one task. Thomas Edison made a statement and he said, **"Many**

Bishop Ben Ugbine

people think that I am smarter than them, no. Other people think about many things all day long but I think about one thing all day long." Your ability to focus on one thing will cause your energy to be focused on it and no doubt you will succeed at it. A scientist who wants to make a new discovery on something important to him often spends hours upon hours on that thing before making any breakthroughs on his discovery. Hard work and dedication is the panacea for success and nobody who is unwilling to devote himself or herself totally to his or her cause would achieve any success. Your labour and effort on what you believe in will determine whether people will honour you or not. Also one could become famous and receive worldwide recognition simply because one is exceptionally good at what one does best. World famous musicians and singers are revered because over time they have dedicated themselves to their work and have produced something of great quality that has brought pleasure and delight to people. Most times your reward in your vocation or craft will be rewarded by how good you have become at it. Nobody in their right mind would want to pay money to go and see a concert when they know that the artist is not proficient in what they do. When somebody has not mastered their craft or art, it leads to embarrassment and disgrace if they try to bring it before the public to see. It does take years and consistent hard work to breed champions.

Champions are not made in a day or in a month. It takes years of consistent practice and hard work to produce a champion. An Olympic champion is not a champion just because they want to be a champion, no; they become champions because of their years of sacrifice and dedication to what they do.

An Olympic swimmer was asked long ago on a television programme how much time she spends in practicing before really becoming an Olympic champion? She responded by saying that she practiced six hours every day for many months. Indeed, that's a lot of time to put on something but you know it brought her a great reward and fame. You will be famous and honoured by how much time you are willing to spend on what you do. Sometimes to achieve success you will have to go through some physical pain and even deny yourself of some things in life. To gain one thing you

How to Succeed in Life

have to sacrifice something else. You cannot be a success of what you do today if all you do is partying all the time and you don't put in quality time to what you want to succeed at. For instance, to be a writer it requires a lot of time alone all by yourself to be able to create something out of nothing. Writing requires quietness and a solitary environment to really bring forth something that would bless or delight others.

Time indeed is a big factor to your success and greatness. The time spent on something would produce the desired outcome a person wants in life. Your time on what you believe in is an investment you are making for your future reward. Most people do not succeed at what they do or involved in simply because adequate time is not given to that very thing. For instance, for somebody to have a successful marriage they need to invest quality time in it. You cannot truly know a person very well if you don't spend quality time with them. Time is an investment that brings tremendous reward and benefits. Your time given to your family or children or business or ministry is an investment you are making for tomorrow. Many marriages and homes have been destroyed today because quality time was not invested into it. What you don't make any investment in don't expect to get any beneficial reward from it.

When an employer employs you to do a job for them they pay you for your time that you put in. You gave them your time and you were rewarded with a salary. If no time was given no money would have been given either.

Acquiring excellence at what you do

Excellence is something we must endeavour to strive for in whatever we do because that is the sure way we can be truly rewarded. The spirit of excellence is a spirit of order. It is the ability to do things effectively, efficiently and appropriately. Anywhere there is a proper arrangement of things it brings harmony, joy and growth. Disorder is the opposite coin of excellence and disorder breeds confusion, stagnation, disintegration and disharmony. God wants us to do everything we do with all of our might, strength and ability and strive for excellence. The spirit of excellence is something we can achieve if we desire it and that is what will attract the world to us. We are not talking of perfection which is an ideal no one can ever achieve but excellence is achievable.

Somebody who tries to achieve perfection in what they do will only end up miserable because a perfectionist is never satisfied with anything. He may have done something spectacular and praise worthy but within himself he feels he has not done enough. On the other hand, a person that strives for excellence will also feel good when they finished what they are doing. Excellence is simply the adequate arrangement of things. An environment where excellence is the order of the day people become happy and others want to associate with it. Nobody wants to be a part of a thing or be in an environment where there is confusion and disorder. Excellence attracts and disorder repels and that is the truth.

It is vitally important that as we are on our way to achieving success in our different field of pursuit, we should desire to achieve excellence in everything we do. The world will not celebrate us if all we desire in life is just to get by in what we do. We must endeavour to give it our all and also settle for 100% and nothing less. A person with the spirit of excellence would always go the extra mile to get things done and they are won't be satisfied until they see that everything is in their right order and proper arrangement.

Your ability to live the life of excellence will make your life happy and less stressful. Disorder brings a lot of stress and if your life is not in order, it will be impossible to experience joy and happiness. When an environment is in order, it removes chaos and confusion and it also produces great pleasure. If excellence can produce pleasure, then of course disorder will invariably produce pain. Nobody wants to experience pain in their life or unhappiness. We all want to experience pleasure and joy and the road to excellence will guarantee just that.

I really do believe that excellence is a spirit that God wants us to appropriate in our lives to get to where He wants us to be. We must avoid every ounce of mediocrity in our lives and do things to the point that men would give glory to God. People are going to be drawn to us when they see order and excellence exhibited in what we do. Your greatness will be seen by how much time and effort you put into what you do and to rise to the top, excellence should be your watchword. Men will honour and celebrate you when the beauty and the glory of God radiates through you because of the spirit of excellence displayed in your life and in what you do.

The spirit of a finisher

Many in their life are not able to achieve success just because they don't know how to finish what they started. You cannot achieve success if you don't have the spirit of a finisher in you. Many people in life starts one thing today and move on to something else without completing what they earlier started and they wonder why their lives are not going anywhere. You must be productive in what you do and you must endeavour to finish one thing before moving on to another. There is no way you are going to achieve happiness and satisfaction if everything you do is unfinished. Completing a task produces great joy in one's life and if all your enterprise is uncompleted, your life will not experience the joy one gets in completing a task.

It is vitally important for you to focus on doing one thing at a time and never leave that thing for something else if it has not been fully completed. Success and progress is achieved in finishing an assignment and any assignment uncompleted is a delay in one's progress in life.

One of the reasons why people don't seem to finish what they started is simply because of temporary obstacles that tend to confront them and then they abandon the task. Obstacles and opposition would certainly come one's way but one must be determined to overcome them and accomplish one's task. Never give up on any project or task simply because of obstacles but always be determined to look for a way to overcome it and finish the task. In fact, this is an area where perseverance and patience would play a big role in our lives. To be able to complete a task successfully, one really needs to have great patience and be able to withstand every obstacle or opposition that may come one's way. If you are not patient with things, it will be extremely had to really be a finisher.

Bishop Ben Ugbine

It is very important for us to finish what we started and not allow discouragement or temporary circumstances to make us to abandon the plan or project. If it's a career you are working on and somehow you got discouraged on the way, try and overcome it and be determined to achieve your dreams. Winners don't quit and quitters don't win and you must be determined to be a winner.

Chapter Eight

REJECT PROCRASTINATION

"Redeeming the time, because the days are evil"
(Eph. 5:16).

Procrastination is the stealer of time and it's a phenomenon that is designed to frustrate your effort to succeed in life. When we put off till tomorrow what should be accomplished today, you tend to forget about them and after a few days if it's not done, it may never be done again. We must endeavour to destroy the spirit of procrastination from our lives and do what should be done today without falling into the temptation of putting it off until the next day. Time is very important in life and any time wasted can never be regained again and once it's gone, it's gone forever.

Procrastination can actually delay your ability to move ahead in life because what is supposed to be finished and completed was never done. Once one has the inspiration to do a thing and it is left undone, that inspiration can be lost forever. For instance, if one has an inspiration to write a song or a play or a story and it is not done at the time the idea came and procrastination sets in, one could lose that idea forever and not have the opportunity to see that idea come to reality. When ideas come to you to do something, it must be acted upon because that thought or idea could be lost forever. Those who are in the creative business know how important ideas are and they are not to be played with. People who are creative or write for a living must always carry with them notebooks to write when they receive inspiration.

Bishop Ben Ugbine

The Spirit world is full of ideas that are released unto us and if we are not sensitive to them they could pass us by. Millions of dollar screen plays or movies have been written because people received inspiration at the spur of the moment. You may even have an idea for a business or to write a book follow it up and don't procrastinate. That idea or thought might very well be what will bring you your success in life.

As human beings, we are crowded with lots of things to do each day and if we don't organize ourselves properly, we could be busy with so much that we don't get things done. Most people working in the office setting sometimes fall into this habit of procrastinating on what ought to be done for the day. Some people tend to pile up things and keep putting them off for the next day, and if more work are received the next day, the work for the previous day could be totally forgotten and left for weeks. We must learn to clear up today's work and if it is not completed, it should be completed the next day before going into new jobs.

When we are conscious of this spirit of procrastination, it completely removes unnecessary stress from our lives. A lot of students tend to be plagued by this spirit of procrastination because of the pressures of work load on them and they tend to put off their project and essays or assignments which has certain deadline until the very last minute. This certainly this could create a lot of stress on one and even though some are able to pull it off even at the very dying minute, but others could be left confused and discouraged at such situations. The best thing to do to avoid this kind of situation is to learn to do things ahead of time even before the deadline and avoid unnecessary stress.

When we allow our lives to be clouded and stressed up, it could affect one's health and lead to high blood pressure, hypertension and even depression. When something that ought to be done is left undone, it gives room for all kinds of mental torment that puts one in a state of panic.

Let us try to simplify our lives by not clouding our lives and do what ought to be done at the right time and not keep on putting off things. The things we put off today could be abandoned for weeks, months and even years and may not get done. Maybe you want to go back to college to earn a degree do it now and don't procrastinate. It is important to take action and follow up what needs to be followed up and get all relevant information that you need to make the decision. Sometimes the fear of not being able to succeed can often paralyze one to put things off but be strong and go ahead and get it done. When you take a step of faith to do what appears difficult, God will enable you and give you the grace to accomplish it. You might be so surprised that what appears to you to be very difficult could even reveal some of your hidden abilities and talents you probably were not aware or conscious about.

The spirit of commitment

Your commitment to your task will be the defining line to how much will come your way. Commitment is the ability to stick to something and bring it into fruition without wavering in one's decision. When a person is not committed to something they scarcely show much interest in that particular thing. Your commitment to your endeavour is indeed what would cause it to be successful. In fact, these days, people really don't want to be committed to things. For instance, a lot of guys are unmarried today because they are afraid to commit themselves to a woman. In any society, organization or institution where commitment is lacking, there would be less achievement.

Indeed, there is power in commitment because things are accomplished easily. The commitment you put into things will cause things to be productive and successful. In a game for instance, if the players are committed to putting in their best to win no doubt they would certainly win. Your dedication to a task would release hidden talents and skills that are yet to be discovered. In fact, anything one gives one's 100% attention to would certainly unmask one's creativity in a way that would really baffle one.

Focused energy

Every single minute of our lives we exert energy on different things as we try to accomplish things for ourselves. Some people's energy is wasted on

Bishop Ben Ugbine

inconsequential things whilst others focus their energy on worthwhile goals and achieve great results. When people's energy are scattered and are not focused on a particular goal, it becomes very difficult for them to achieve substantial result.

Energy is a concentrated force that causes things to happen and when this force is fully focused on one thing, it creates an intensity that produces Satisfactory results. We need to focus all our energy on a chosen goal or career or dream and let the intensity of our focus begin to generate passion that can make things happen for us. This energy that we possess in us is a great spiritual power indeed that if directed accurately on the right things, it would cause supernatural things to happen. Those who are spiritually disciplined channel this energy into healing and rendering spiritual help to people.

It is important that we channel this energy in us into things that would benefit the world as opposed to using it to bring destruction to people's lives. There are people who concentrate all their energy into planning and scheming evil against other people but that is energy wrongly directed. Some people put all their energy in doing charitable work and this brings tremendous benefit to society which in turn brings much joy into their lives.

Whatever your calling or vocation is, your energy should be geared towards benefiting your community or society and allow God to use you as a blessing. We are all here on earth to carry out an assignment for God and it is important to recognize what it is and devote ourselves completely to doing just that. Your joy and happiness would be increased when you do what you are designed to do and you do it with all of your might and energy.

Divine energy is the source of power on earth and it is through this divine energy that our lives are sustained. God is the substance of all forms and His energy gives life to all sentient beings. We as the creation of God, have all His characteristics and abilities imbedded in us that can enable us to achieve great feats in life. This energy of God dwells in us and this energy or power or spirit can energize us to exhibit the fruits and the gifts of the Spirit. God has given us the power or the anointing to heal the

How to Succeed in Life

sick, raise the dead and do phenomenal things here on earth. When we prepare ourselves as usable channels to reach mankind, His power or divine energy will radiate and flow through us to help the afflicted. God is always looking for holy vessels to flow through and His power is unlimited and it can heal and set the captives free.

God's anointing power or divine energy can set the captives free and release them from the bondages of the demonic forces. If you are sick right now let that power flow into you to destroy every demonic seed that has been planted in your life to harm you. God's spirit is able to destroy every yoke of bondage and give you the divine health that is your portion.

God has made us as healing agents in the world and that healing can be effected in different form. Your channel of healing can be healing emotionally wounded souls and for someone else it could be a channel for psychological healing or healing spiritually wounded souls. There are countless people out there in the world suffering from one predicament or the other and God wants us to use His divine energy or power to help them. When we become a blessing to people, God causes us to experience His spiritual joy in our lives. And as we sow good works and good deeds into people's lives, so will God allows others to do onto us.

God's gifts abound in all of us and we have to use it according to the measure of grace He has released upon us. His grace is sufficient for us to do great things. When His power or energy or anointing flows through you no doubt you become His messenger to the world to cause healing and deliverance to take place. Of course many are bound by the forces of darkness in different areas of their lives and we need to set them free. Many are bound in their marriages and others are bound in their minds and emotions and they need the deliverance of God. Some are also bound sexually and this power of God can truly set them free to be what God has ordained them to be. If the son of man shall set you free, you shall be free indeed (John 8:36). When His power loses you then you will be free to enjoy His blessings in your life and do what you want to do. Indeed, we are no longer under the bondages of the enemy but we are free and whole in God.

CHAPTER NINE

THE I CAN PHILOSOPHY

"I can do all things through Christ who strengtheneth me" (Phil. 4:13).

You can make it in life if you think you can. The word can't have actually limited many on their pathway to achieving things for themselves. When you say you can't, you stop yourself from moving forward and progressing in your life and what you want to achieve then becomes impossible. It's important to strike the 'T' off the word can't and then begin to say to yourself I can. Let nobody ever tell you that you can't be what you want to be or achieve what you want to achieve.

The only person that can really stop you from achieving greatness is you and nobody else. It doesn't matter how limited your background is or what people have said you couldn't be, brush it off and say to yourself **'I can make it and nothing can stop me.'**

When this word 'I can' can really register in you, then you will become unstoppable and you can truly conquer the world. One of my favourite men in the entire world is Benjamin Franklin because he achieved phenomenal things in his life in spite of his poor background and limited education. He had only two years of education in his life but he never allowed that to hinder him but he believed that he could achieve his dream and he became one of the most famous men in American history.

How to Succeed in Life

I want you to know that you can make it and you have what it takes to make it. Don't look down on yourself and don't judge yourself by what people think of you rather believe that you can and certainly you will. In short, anytime you feel your confidence is waning just repeat over and over to yourself that you can make it. When you say it over and over again to yourself your mind will register it and you will begin to feel your confidence rise and before you know it, what appears impossible will become possible.

In your road to achieving your goals or dreams never allow anybody to discourage you or talk you out of what you can achieve. The world is before you and all you need to do is to be determined concerning what you want and go for it. You certainly can make it and I need to keep saying it to you until it can finally register in your mind. Greatness begins with assurance and when you are assured of something your confidence grows and your ability to do that thing becomes possible. You have a God of possibilities and He can assist you to make your dream come true. **"With God all things are possible"** (Luke 1:37).

Some people, in life have had a very traumatized childhood experience that has left some negative tapes in their minds that keeps playing over and over again to paralyze them from moving ahead in life. If you grew up in a home where your parents kept telling you that you are a good for nothing person or that your life will not amount to anything, after awhile, you begin to believe it as true. When those words have taken a strong root in your mind, they tend to hinder you in life because anytime you want to do something for yourself suddenly here comes those tapes telling you that you can't. It is not easy to erase those tapes but with God all things are possible. What you need to do in this situation is use powerful affirmative words to override those childhood tapes. If you keep saying to yourself, **'I can make it with God on my side',** then if this is done over a long period of time, those other tapes would have less power over you.

Usually our past tends to affect our now. What was sown years back can begin to affect our lives today and even into the future if nothing is done about it. Our lives are made up of different experiences that run from childhood into adulthood and every problem we tend to have in our lives is a childhood problem left unaddressed. When our childhood problems are not dealt with it becomes a repeated pattern that affects our adult lives. When a child is made to feel insecure or ashamed, it causes a psychological trauma to take place which leaves an imprint in the mind that keep on reoccurring in one's life. A child that is made to feel insecure will develop fear and lack of trust in people and this can even be carried on into their married life. If a person was insecure from childhood and grows up to be an adult and marries, nothing his or her spouse does will ever make them secure. This is where therapy comes in to visit the childhood experience and confront the situation that began that insecurity in the first place. So our lives experiences are really left-overs from our childhood days that have left traumatic experiences in us.

I strongly believe that you can break whatever traumatic pattern you are faced with in your life. It all boils down to the 'I can philosophy'. If you think you can break the pattern and be free from those ugly childhood experiences, you certainly can. You don't have to allow the limitations of your past to affect your bright and glorious future. It is important that you take 100% control of your life and decide to make a change in your life. Yes, what has happened has happened and that we cannot undo but you can take responsibility for what happens to you hereafter.

It doesn't matter what your parents or people may have done to you or said to you that you couldn't help, but right now put a stop to it and decide to move on with your life. You can decide to do two things. It is either you will continue to feel bitter and resentful about it, or you can choose to make a turn around and put all that behind you. It's important that you put the past behind you and take responsibility of your now and your future. Your future is pregnant with greatness and there are more ahead of you than behind you. Your past you cannot change or undo but your future you can grasp hold of and make something beautiful out of it. You certainly can make it and rise up now from every pity party and be the person you always wanted to be.

How to Succeed in Life

Press on to obtain your dream

Your dream is realizable but you have to press on to obtain it. God has already blessed us with all spiritual blessings in the heavenly places before the foundation of the world but we have to overcome all the negative forces of the enemy and obtain it. The fact that God has already blessed us does not mean that everything is just going fall down on our lap; no, we have to press on and obtain it. In fact, the forces of darkness are doing everything possible in their power to stop us from receiving what God has already given us from the foundation of the world but we have to put up a spiritual fight to overcome them. The bible says we are not wrestling against flesh and blood but against spiritual forces. **"For we wrestle not against flesh and blood, but against principalities, against powers, against the rulers of darkness of this world, against spiritual wickedness in high places"** (Eph. 6:12).

There are contrary forces always trying to prevent us from enjoying the blessings of God but we have to stand on the truth of God's word concerning our blessings and appropriate them in our lives. We are heirs to God's throne and everything in His kingdom belongs to us. Indeed, we are supposed to enjoy the full blessings of God and if the enemy is stopping you from doing that, you have to take authority over him and enjoy your blessings.

We need to press on, in other words we have to put up a spiritual fight against the forces of darkness and let them know that we have authority over them. God has put every demonic force under the feet of Christ and we need to exert that authority in our lives as well. **"And hath put all things under his feet, and gave him to be the head over all things to the church"** (Eph. 1:22).

The devil and his forces are going about trying to derail and abort people's destiny and make them feel hopeless and forlorn, and trying to deprive us from seeing the fullness of God in our lives. When God says we are blessed that's what He means and nothing can change that. Your blessings are not determined by a person or a human being rather they are determined by

Bishop Ben Ugbine

God Himself. So don't allow anything or demonic forces to stop you from receiving your full blessings in life. Indeed, you are blessed and you need to believe that. Your present situation or circumstance might not reflect that you are blessed but don't look at that just believe what God has decreed and walk in it.

No matter what we face in life, we have to press on and obtain what is before us. The Apostle Paul made this statement, **"Not as though I had already attained, either were already perfect: but I follow after, if that I may apprehend that for which also I am apprehended of Christ Jesus. Brethren, I count not myself to have apprehended: but this one thing I do, forgetting those things which are behind, and reaching forth unto those things which are before, I press towards the mark for the prize of the high calling of God in Christ Jesus"** (Phil. 3:12-14).

Life is about pressing ahead to obtain or win. For someone to press they have to have a force coming up against them and to be victorious they have to press ahead. You need to press to obtain what God has ahead for you. When we press towards the mark of the high calling or towards our goals and dreams, something supernatural takes place to give us the victory.

Indeed, this is not the time to be complacent or say I've made it no rather we have to understand that there are more battles ahead and there are more victories to be achieved. The spirit of complacency is the spirit of stagnation. Where you are right now, isn't really where God wants you to be and He will give you more victories if you endeavour to press on. The scripture we quoted above reveals to us that Paul wasn't complacent rather he chose to put the past behind and reach forth to what was ahead – that is he was reaching for the prize of the high calling of God. There is a high prize ahead of us and a greater reward that we need to obtain. Your yesterday's victory is for yesterday and you need new victories today. We move from faith to faith and from glory to glory and we need to be forward moving. Every conquest we've had in the past should as a matter of fact spur us on for more achievement. Success is really your daily conquest and when accumulated leads to greater success. We must resist every spirit that would tell us that we have received everything we need to receive. In short,

How to Succeed in Life

God blesses us so that we can also be a blessing to others and indeed there are so many people in the world today that are really in need and we need to be a blessing to them as well.

We need to bear in mind that we are here on earth to complete an assignment for God and that assignment must be fulfilled. You can be whatever you want to be and nothing in this world can stop you and so run and be a success story. You are well able to do it and God's grace is upon you to make it happen.

CHAPTER TEN

BELIEVE IN GOD TO SUCCEED

"Let not your heart be troubled' ye believe in God, believe also in me" (Jn. 14:1).

"And Jesus answering saith unto them, Have faith in God. For verily I say unto you, That whosoever shall say unto this mountain, Be thou removed, and be thou cast into the sea: and shall not doubt in his heart, but shall believe that those things which he saith shall come to pass; he shall have whatsoever he saith. Therefore, I say unto you, What things soever ye desire, when ye pray, believe that ye receive them, and ye shall have them" (Mark 11:22-24).

God is the source of life and He is the creator of the ends of the earth. He said let there be and there was. In fact, God calls the things that be not as though they were (Rom. 4:17b). God created all forms by the spoken word and His words were so powerful that it brought forth what He desired. We need to understand that words are spirit and they carry divine mandate and bring things into manifestation. Our words create things whether we know it or not. Good words produce good fruit and bad words produce bad fruits.

If we need to ride high in life, then we definitely have to believe in God to make it happen for us. We fail woefully in life because we tend to depend solely on ourselves and not in God. God is the strength of our lives and

How to Succeed in Life

He knows the beginning from the end and also the heart of the king is in His hand and He can turn it around to favour one.

The scripture in John 14:1 encourages us to believe in God. Actually our miracle begins when we believe in God. Unbelief can hinder us from receiving. Believing in God is really having faith in Him and knowing that He is able to do what He said He would do. God's word cannot return unto Him void it must accomplish something. **"So shall my word be that goeth forth out of my mouth: it shall not return unto me void, but it shall accomplish that which I please, and it shall prosper in the thing whereto I sent it"** (Isaiah 55:11).

We need to understand that God's word is God and He values His word more than His name. **"For thou hast magnified thy word above all thy name"** (Psalm 138:2b). God's word is life and it is truth and it can cause great and mighty things to happen to us if we believe it.

With God on your side, it can cause impossible things to happen for you. There are certain things that are impossible with men but not with God. There are gigantic projects you probably want to achieve right now and you really don't have the resources to make things happen for you but if you will believe in God to supply, He will provide all the resources you need. Your God is a mighty God and He expects us to have big dreams and mighty projects that He can help us to accomplish. It doesn't matter the size of your dream or project it cannot move God. In fact, God can do far more than we can ask or think. **"Now unto him that is able to do exceeding abundantly above all that we ask or think, according to the power that worketh in us"** (Eph. 3:20).

When we come to God we must believe that He is able to do what we ask of Him. God is like the ocean and the ocean can handle any capacity that you bring before it. Indeed, God likes it when He sees His children believing Him for great things. Heaven is not limited and the bigger our dreams and visions, the more we are able to help the less privileged in our society.

When Jesus spoke to the tree in Mark chapter eleven, the tree began to wither and die. He spoke that no man should eat fruit from the tree no more forever and it dried up. When Peter and the disciples saw it, they were amazed and they drew Jesus' attention to it but He told them to have faith in God. Faith in God is the starting point for miracles to happen. He said to them that if they can have faith they can say to the mountain be thou removed and cast into the sea and if they don't doubt in their heart concerning what they have said, it will come to pass. So whatever we desire when we pray we should believe that we receive them and they will surely come to pass.

Your faith in God will no doubt put you in a place to see mighty things come to pass. Develop a partnership with God and let Him be the CEO of everything you do and you will see it blossom and become very productive and fruitful. Both you and God cannot fail at all and that needs to sink deeply into one's mind.

In short, when God is on your side, then the whole world would definitely be with you. God knows your needs even before you pray and you don't need to remind Him of anything in your life. Even the heart of the king can be turned to favour you and God can speak to anybody who can lift you up to lift you up. In short for us to ride high in life, we need to be connected to the right people for them to show us favour and open some doors for us and when we link up with God, He will make it come true for us. We really don't need everybody to like us but the right person and the right person will be the link you need to make things happen for you. Nobody indeed is an island and nobody can succeed all by themselves but having God as your best friend and partner is really all you need to succeed. God knows the right person for you and He will schedule a divine appointment for you to meet that person and then things will begin to happen for you thereafter.

Your trust in God

Our trust in God should be total and complete and when we do that we can go to bed and not worry about anything. Many people have really paralyzed themselves because what they should have given to God to handle they have chosen to handle by themselves. God can take care of

How to Succeed in Life

what you commit into His hands and whatever we take care of by ourselves we will lose. When our trust is completely rested on God then we can go to bed and sleep peacefully. God gives His beloved sleep but anxiety and worry is the portion of the unbeliever. **"Except the LORD build the house, they labour in vain that build it: except the LORD keep the city, the watchman walketh but in vain. It is vain for you to rise up early, to sit up late, to eat the bread of sorrows: for so he giveth his beloved sleep"** (Psalm 127:1&2).

Today anxiety has really weighed down many and life seems so unbelievable to them but we don't need to be anxious of anything at all. Anxiety is only a sign that we don't need to be anxious of anything at all. And it is also a sign that we don't have implicit trust in God to help and deliver us. **"Be careful for nothing; but in everything by prayer and supplication with thanksgiving let your requests be made known unto God. And the peace of God, which passeth all understanding, shall keep your hearts and minds through Christ Jesus"** (Phil. 4:6&7).

Anxiety can kill and also destroy one's life and we don't need that to happen to us at all. No matter the troubles you might be going through right now, trust God to see you through. You might even be going through a very hard time in your marriage right now but if you can trust God and pray, He will work things out alright. Maybe you might be feeling right now that your marriage is about to end up in divorce but let me assure you that nothing is too difficult for God to handle. If you can trust Him totally and completely, He will definitely bring peace back into your marriage.

God's peace will always keep you through unkeepable times. When the peace of God rests in your heart nothing you go through will even border you. In fact, God's peace will comfort and uphold you in your storm. You know in the middle of every storm there is a place of great calmness and we need to let God show us those calm areas in every storm we might be faced with.

It is important to note that no storm lasts forever and your storm will certainly pass and you will begin to experience peace in your life. Indeed,

Bishop Ben Ugbine

your storm or storms are only a sign that the hand of God is upon you. You know the devil only attacks people that he knows will amount to much and so if you are going through some storms right now, know that your life will definitely amount to much. Even when it seems like your boat is sinking in the ocean of life right now, just trust God and He will never let you be moved. **"O my God, I trust in thee, let me not be ashamed, let not mine enemies triumph over me"** (Psalm 25:2). And also Psalm 27:1 says, **"The LORD is my light and my salvation; whom shall I fear? the LORD is the strength of my life; of whom shall I be afraid."**

God is your protection and you will not sink in life but you will overcome and become more than a conqueror. And whatever you are passing through right now will soon calm down and you will see your way through again. Hope thou in God and you will yet praise Him again. All is not lost with you but you have every cause to praise God again. **"Why art thou cast down, O my soul? And why art thou disquieted within me? Hope thou in God; for I shall yet praise him, who is the health of my countenance, and my God"** (Psalm 42:11).

Overcoming fiery trials

Our trust in God must be higher when we are going through fiery trials. Fiery trials are trials that can kill you or leave scarred for life. Life is full of ups and downs and every now and then we go through fiery trials and that trial could be in your marriage, job, business, ministry or your health. But when you find yourself in a fiery trial, just remember that you will not be burnt but God will deliver you and you will come out unhurt.

Shedrach, Mechach, and Abednego went through a fiery trial but they trusted in their God and He delivered them. They had an encounter with Nebudchadnezzar who wanted them to worship his god of idol but they refused and choose rather to be put in their fiery furnace. They were not moved by the threat rather they choose to trust in their God to deliver them and He did. **"Nebudchadnezzar spake and said unto them, Is it true, O Shedrach, Meshach, and Abednego, do not ye serve my gods, nor worship the golden image which I have set up? Now if ye be ready**

How to Succeed in Life

that at what time ye hear the sound of the cornet, flute, harp, sackbut, psalmtery, and musick, ye fall down and worship the image which I made; well, but if ye worship not, ye shall be cast the same hour into the midst of a burning fiery furnace; and who is that God that shall deliver you out of my hand? Shedrach, Meshach, and Abednego, answered and said to the king, O Nebudchadnezzar, we are not careful to answer thee in this matter. If it be so, our God whom we serve is able to deliver us from the burning fiery furnace, and he will deliver us out of thine hand, O King. But if not, be it known unto thee, O King, that we will not serve thy gods, nor worship the golden image thou hast set up" (Dan. 3:1418).

Nebudchadnezzar was furious with Shedrach, Meshach, and Abednego and they were cast into the fiery furnace. In fact, the furnace was so hot that the men that cast them in were killed by the fire but Shedrach, Meshach and Abednego were unhurt by the fire. When Nebudchadnezzar saw it he was surprised and he commanded them to be brought out and the king made a decree throughout the land for everyone to serve the God of Shedrach, Meshach and Abednego. **"Then Nebudchadnezzar spake, and said, Blessed be the God of Shedrach, Meshach, and Abednego who hath sent his angel, and delivered his servants that trusted in him, and have changed the king's word, and yielded their bodies, that they might not serve nor worship any god, except their own God. Therefore, I make a decree, That every people, nation, and language, which speak anything amiss against the God of Shedrach, Meshach, and Abednego, shall be cut in pieces, and their houses shall be made a dunghill because there is no other God that can deliver after this sort. Then the king promoted Shedrach, Meshach, and Abednego, in the province of Babylon"** (Dan. 3:28-30).

Promotion always comes after a great trial in your life. In fact, anytime God wants to take you to another level of blessing He will also allow the enemy to attack you with an overwhelming attack but always know that you will come out unhurt and greatly blessed. If your life is going through a fiery furnace right now, don't let it overwhelm you just trust in God and He will surely deliver you. **"Yea, though I walk through the valley of**

Bishop Ben Ugbine

the shadow of death, I will fear no evil: for thou art with me; thy rod and thy staff they comfort me. Thou preparest a table before me in the presence of mine enemies: thou anointest my head with oil; my cup runneth over. Surely goodness and mercy shall follow me all the days of my life' and I will dwell in the house of the LORD forever" (Psalm 23:4-6).

God always prepares a table for you in the midst of your enemies even when your enemies are trying to kill you. He wants you to know that no matter what trial you are facing right now you will come out very blessed and those who have despised you will honour you and nobody can be against you. **"What shall we say then to these things? If God be for us, who can be against us?"** (Rom. 8:31). God is on your side and nobody can be against you. In fact, they would try to be against you but all their attempts will be frustrated by God. So child of God be encouraged and know that God is certainly on your side and He will bring you through alright. Be rest assured that you and God are unbeatable team and as a result you need to trust Him completely and totally and don't ever waver in your confident walk with Him.

Chapter Eleven

BELIEVE IN YOURSELF

"Cast not away therefore your confidence which hath great recompence of reward" (Hebs 10:35).

You really have to believe in yourself that you have what it takes to make it in life. If no one believes in you at least you can believe in yourself. When you have confidence in yourself it can cause you to achieve a lot in life. Nothing in life can be achieved when one has a low self-esteem about oneself. Low self-esteem can truly hinder you from going into the world and making it. Most people lose their confidence because of the negative words they always hear about themselves. When low self-esteem sets in one's life, one tends to believe other people more than oneself. Low self-esteem could come about in one's life for a number of reasons but the bottom line is that it takes a confident person to be successful and we need to work on our self-esteem if we intend to soar in life.

Once we can dare to believe in ourselves then we will develop the skills and abilities that will enable us to achieve our dreams. The world is looking for confident men and woman that can face the challenges of life and make a great impact in their organization or society. As a matter fact, there is hardly anything one wants to do that doesn't require confidence. That's the reason why the bible encourages us not to cast our confidence away because it has great reward. When we are confident we become bold and

Bishop Ben Ugbine

assertive and we are not afraid to speak our minds or make our point of view known.

Assertive people usually move ahead faster than less assertive people. We all need a certain amount of belief in ourselves to rise to the top in whatever strata of life we may find ourselves.

Walking in confidence requires knowledge of oneself and what one does. Let's talk first about the knowledge of oneself. It is important to know yourself very well because that will enable you to ascertain what you have the ability to do and what your weaknesses are. The great Socrates made a statement and he said, 'Know thyself.' Self-knowledge is very paramount in moving forward to do something. When people don't know who they are and what they are all about, they waste their precious time in pursuing frivolous and inconsequential goals or carrier and even engaged themselves in the wrong business too. Life is not really about trying different things out to see if they can work for us, no, it's about knowing and doing what we are really good at.

When I know my weaknesses and my strength, it will afford me the knowledge to know what area not to focus on. Low self-esteem comes when our weaknesses overwhelm our strength and when that happens, it weakens our ability to do things.

Knowing yourself would put you in a favourable situation to know your dreams and aspirations and pursue them accordingly. You are the express image of God and He has imbedded some dreams and aspirations in the inside of you to carry out a divine plan for Him. When God created you He put every valuable gift and skills in you that would enable you to carry out your assignment effectively. What you are doing right now was ordained by God Himself and He knows you are well suited for your assignment and well able to do it as well.

When you understand who you are and what your potentials are, there is no human being on earth that can intimidate you or stop you from fulfilling your assignment. Every one of us as human beings are different in our human makeup and God put something in every one of us that the

How to Succeed in Life

other person may not necessarily have. Because your assignment is different from mine, it then requires us to be interdependent upon one another for the fulfilment our individual assignment in life.

There are things in me that you require that would keep you going in life hence we are somewhat in need of each other. Nobody was made to be completely independent from another person. We are all involved in an intricate web of mutuality and what affects you affects me. This is simply because we are all divinely connected and flow from one Omnipotent source which is God. We were made by God in such a way that we are all hooked up with Him for our strength and sustenance and we can't truly function without His divine intervention and help.

When we truly understand our make-up and source, it should gives us the awareness that God has endowed us with supernatural strength to do things. This strength and ability we possess of God can only be known when we are in a cordial relationship with Him. This is the strength Paul referred to as, '**When I am weak then I am strong** (2 Cor. 12:10). Believing in yourself is simply bringing your mind to the fact that God gave you His divine strength and ability which should be used by acknowledging Him. We all need this divine strength and ability to achieve things that ordinarily we can't achieve by ourselves.

From childhood when we were born, we were supposed to learn intuitively and grow from within but the world has instituted an educational system that is designed to discourage intuitive learning rather one is deprogrammed with a system that wants you to learn outwardly. Education is good and we need it but we all need to learn from within. That's the reason why Jesus said, **"The kingdom of God is within you"** (Luke 17:21). God's kingdom is not a heavenly location rather it is a spiritual environment where the fullness of God can be realized.

We need to be drawn to the Spirit of God within us to impart unto us the wisdom of God to achieve great feats. Until we understand this inner spiritual environment, we will be depending on the help of man when we should be depending on an inward divine power. When we can grapple this fact, we can walk on water like Jesus or call fire down from heaven like Elijah or part the Red Sea like Moses. Realistically speaking, when we know the source from whence we came, it will cause you to believe in yourself to the point that nothing and I mean absolutely nothing, can really stop you in life. When we don't know this, fear sets in and we become less confident in being successful and achieving great success in life. Why is it so important for us to believe in ourselves? Believing in yourself is not talking about self-reliance, no that's not what I'm talking about. Self-reliance as a matter of fact is the easiest way for a person to be completely destroyed. Nobody is self-reliant since we all are interdependent upon one another and also depended upon God. By believing in yourself, I am actually talking about being cognizant of the fact that you have a divine ability within you that can propel you to succeed or make it in life. This divine ability came from God and when we are cognizant of it, the reward can be very phenomenal indeed.

Your spiritual power

The story of Samson in the bible is very unique because it reveals a unique strength in a human vessel. Samson was able to do things beyond any human capability because he tapped into his divine inner power. Indeed, we may not necessarily have the physical strength of Samson but we possess it spiritually.

The power of God is within you and you are more of a spiritual being than physical. When we see ourselves as mere physical beings, then we are limited to this inner power of God that I'm referring to. Jesus realized this inner power and He used it to do incredible miracles. He was able to heal the sick, raise the dead and even feed five thousand people with five loaves of bread and two fishes. In fact, He was also able ask Peter to launch out into the deep for a great catch because He was operating under this divine power that He possessed in the inside of Him (Luke 5).

In all honesty, we are all messengers of God whether we realize it or not. As messengers of God, we are endowed with divine ability to carry out God's will and purpose. The reason why incredible miracles are not taking

How to Succeed in Life

place the way they should is simply because we have limited ourselves and we are walking as mere men without any spiritual power. If every one of us will tap into this spiritual power we will open blind eyes, raise the dead and do wonders upon the face of the earth. God is constantly looking for men and women who will walk in this divine power. This power is not the exclusive preserve of only a few people, no, it is meant for every one of us. Anybody can be used of God if we can tap into that spiritual source of power and use it to be a blessing to people and to the glory of God.

God wants us to walk in this spiritual power. As a matter of fact, when we walk in this spiritual power, we will rise above sickness and disease. In the spiritual realm, there is no such thing as sickness and disease but eternity. Everything exists in eternity because God is eternal. Sickness and disease exists only in the physical body or realm and this is as a result of us believing in two powers. If we believe in the power of God, then there would be no sickness but if we believe in material medica, then sickness and decay and death will set in. From God's vantage point there is no such thing as sickness, death or disease. These are only beliefs in human minds and this has held them in bondage and in captivity. That's why Jesus could see the blind and asked them to receive their sight or look at the paralyzed and say to them take your bed and begin to walk.

Jesus as a matter of fact was always operating in the fullness of the Spirit. When we live above sin and give ourselves wholly to God, we become full of the spirit and we can do supernatural work for God. Living in the physical realm or life is much more limiting and devoid of power but if we operate from the spiritual realm, every natural law will be obedient to the power of God.

God functions through you for the good of mankind and we are God's healing balm to the world. Actually God is constantly looking for men and women who will demonstrate His power to the world. Indeed, we can become healing channels to God if we will get away from the pulls of mundane life and concentrate ourselves for holy service. God can use you and you have to believe that He can and tap into the fire that is within you. When we give ourselves to fasting and prayers and remove ourselves

Bishop Ben Ugbine

from all sexual sins and immoral acts, we truly will see the glory of God manifested through us to mankind.

We have all heard of men like Smith Wigglesworth, T.L. Osborn, Oral Roberts, Lester Summerall, Kathryn Kuhlman and Benny Hinn, just to name a few, who walked in this supernatural power of God. God can use any vessel if that vessel is made ready for service. We have to believe that we can do supernatural works and God would use us accordingly.

Chapter Twelve

TAKE THE BULL BY THE HORN

"Behold, I give unto you power to tread on serpents and scorpions, and over all the power of the enemy: and nothing shall by any means hurt you" (Luke 10:19).

Life is full of challenges and there are many things that are really frightening to be engaged in that truly demands courage and strong determination. The fear of failure or the fear of not making it alone can be very frightening and intimidating to undertake. Realistically speaking, there is hardly any person in life that doesn't feel some amount of fear when they try to embark on something new. It is good to feel some amount of fear to help propel you to take the plunge. Life's challenges are like a diver who has to take a plunge from his diving board into the water and this does need tremendous courage and self determination to do.

The only way to get something done is really to do it. Feel the fear and do it anyway. Don't allow the fear of failure to stop you. Go ahead and get the job done. We have to take the bull by the horn in spite of our fears and intimidations. Our fears are really unfounded and if we will develop some courage then we can do what seems so difficult and challenging. What separates true champions from others is the fact that champions tend to rise above their fears by taking the challenges that come their way and use them to their own advantage.

Bishop Ben Ugbine

Actually one can truly entertain some fears especially when they are trying to begin something from the scratch. For instance, someone starting a new business is always afraid of what the outcome of the business might be. Certainly we cannot predict what will happen in the future but we can trust God and get it started anyway. As one starts the business or project, different questions that would arise will certainly answer themselves. Somebody building a house for instance may not know exactly how everything might turn out until everything is fully completed. Answers would always come to every question as we move along. Every question certainly has an answer even if the answer is not made manifest. If we search hard and long enough every answer would reveal itself to us.

The unpredictability of the future is really holding people from taking the bull by the horn and do what they have in their mind to do. If you are waiting for a time that you will get the goose bumps to do something, you may not have it but you have to go on and begin what you have planned to do. Sometimes in life we need to take some risk and attempt what looks frightening and challenging. Without risk taking, there can be no gain and for you to make a headway in life, you need to take some risk.

The story of the four leprous men in 2 Kings chapter seven shows what can happen when we take risk in life. The four lepers were coming from a very disadvantaged point and everything was up against them. They were lepers and were ostracized and again there was famine in Samaria and also they were outside the City gate, and if they attempt to go inside there was hunger there and again the Syrians their enemies were equally ahead of them. Everything looked bleak for them but they chose to take risk by moving ahead to the Syrian camp rather than going back into the City where there was no food. Let's hear what they said to themselves. **"And there were four leprous men at the entering in of the gate: and they said one to another, Why sit we here until we die? If we say, We will enter into the City, then the famine is in the City, and we shall die there: and if we sit still here, we die also. Now therefore come, and let us fall unto the host of the Syrians: if they save us alive, we shall live; and if they kill us, we shall but die. And they rose up in the twilight, to go unto the camp of the Syrians: and when they were**

How to Succeed in Life

come to the uttermost part of the camp of Syria, behold, there was no man there. For the Lord had made the host of the Syrians to hear a noise of chariots and a noise of horses, even the noise of a great host: and they said one to another, Lo, the king of Israel hath hired against us the kings of the Hittites, and the kings of the Egyptians, to come upon us. Wherefore they arose and fled in the twilight, and left their tents, and their horses, and their asses, even the camp as it was and fled for their life. And when these lepers came to the uttermost part of the camp, they went into one tent, and did eat and drink, and carried thence silver, and gold, and raiment, and went and hid it; and came again and entered into another tent, and carried thence also, and went and hid it" (2 Kings 7:3-8).

These four lepers took risk and God gave them victory by creating confusion in the minds of the Syrians to hear a mighty sound of chariots and horses coming against them and they fled and left all their goods for these four leprous men. If they had remained were they were because of fear obviously they would have perished with hunger but they decided to take the risk and they became blessed.

You really cannot see great things happen for you until you put your fears and worries aside and take that risk and do what you want for your life. Only those who are courageous and brave can really eat of the good of the land. Life's challenges are indeed quite enormous but somehow we have to take the plunge. Many are standing by the pool of life vacillating in their minds whether to take the plunge or retreat.

You have to move forward to really make it. When the children of Israel were faced with the Red Sea, God did not tell them to retreat but to move forward. Victory is ahead of you and not behind you. In fact, when Moses cried to the Lord about what to do He instructed Moses to tell the people to go forward. **"And the LORD said unto Moses, Wherefore criest thou unto me? Speak unto the children of Israel, that they go forward. But lift thou up thy rod, and stretch out thine hand over the sea, and divide it: and the children of Israel shall go on dry ground through the midst of the sea"** (Ex. 14:15&16).

Bishop Ben Ugbine

The children of Israel were afraid because behind them were the Egyptians coming in the chariots to take them back to Egypt and in front of them was the Red Sea yet God told them to move forward. When God told them to move forward, He wasn't trying to drown them in the Red Sea rather He wanted to show forth His miracle power in the midst of their terrible problems. God instructed Moses to use his rod to part the Sea and when he did, the children of Israel walked on dry ground through the midst of the Red Sea.

God had already told them to stand still and see His salvation which He will show them today. He told them that the Egyptians they see today they will see them again no more forever. Indeed, the Egyptians soldiers were drowned in the same Red Sea that delivered the children of Israel. In times of great fear if we trust God and do what He says we should do, certainly He will give us the victory.

The Lion's den

The devil and his demonic forces are really bent on destroying lives and eat up people's flesh. In fact, the devil will do anything or go to any length to destroy lives. **"Be sober, be vigilant; because your adversary the devil, as a roaring lion, walketh about, seeking whom he may devour. Whom resist steadfast in the faith"** (1 Pet. 5:8&9).

It is important to resist the forces of darkness and not allow them to throw you into the den of the demonic lions to destroy your flesh. There are demonic powers who feed on human flesh and drink human blood and they are no mercy killers and they would kill whatever they can lay their hands on. The devil is always walking about looking for scape-goats to devour and you must protect yourself and your household not to fall into his trap. **"When the wicked, even mine enemies and my foes, came upon me to eat up my flesh, they stumbled and fell"** (Psalm 27:2). And Isaiah 49:26 says, **"And I will feed them that oppress thee with their own flesh, and they shall be drunken with their own blood, as with sweet wine: and all flesh shall know that I the LORD am thy saviour and thy Redeemer, the mighty One of Jacob."**

How to Succeed in Life

There are situations that we face in life that looks like we've been thrown into the lion's den for demonic lions to eat up our flesh. The forces of darkness only want to destroy us but we must know that we are under the protection of God. In the book of Daniel we were told how Daniel the Hebrew boy overcame the lion's den when he was thrown in for praying to his God. Daniel was somebody that prayed thrice a day to his God and out of jealousy his conspirators reported him to the king and asked the king to make a decree that nobody should serve or bow down to another god in thirty days. Of course Daniel was not moved by this decree but continued to pray to his God.

In fact, Daniel opened his window so wide for his conspirators to hear and see him pray. **"All the presidents of the kingdom, the governors and the princes, the counselors, and the captains, have consulted together to establish a royal statute, and to make a firm decree, that whosoever shall ask a petition of any God or man for thirty days, save of thee, O King, he shall be cast into the den of lions. Now, O King, establish the decree, and sign the writing, that it be not changed, according to the law of the Medes and Persians, which altered not. Wherefore King Darius signed the writing and the decree. Now when Daniel knew that the writing was signed, he went into his house; and his windows being opened in his chamber towards Jerusalem, he kneeled upon his knees three times a day, and prayed, and gave thanks before his God, as he did a foretime"** (Dan. 6:7-10).

Daniel disobeyed the decree and chose rather to trust his God for deliverance instead. He was cast into the lion's den but Daniel was not hurt by the lions. **"Then the king commanded, and they brought Daniel, and cast him into the den of lions. Now the king spake and said unto Daniel, Thy God whom thou servest continually, he will deliver thee"** (Dan. 6:16).

The king loved Daniel very much but because of the decree he signed, he had no choice than to cast Daniel into the lion's den but the king knew that Daniel's God was going to deliver him anyway. God indeed sent His angels and they shut the lion's mouth so that Daniel could not be hurt.

Bishop Ben Ugbine

When the king found out that Daniel was not hurt, he asked for Daniel to be brought out and all his conspirators and their families were cast into the lion's den and they were all consumed even before their body could touch the ground.

"Then the King arose very early in the morning, and went in haste unto the den of lion's. And when he came to the den, he cried with a lamentable voice unto Daniel: and the king spake and said to Daniel, O Daniel, servant of the living God, is thy God, whom thou servest continually able to deliver thee from the lions? Then said Daniel, unto the king, O King, live forever. My God hath sent his angels, and hath shut the lions mouths, that they have not hurt me: for as much as before him innocency was found in me; and also before thee, O King, have I done no hurt. Then was the King exceeding glad for him, and commanded that they should take Daniel up out of the den. So Daniel was taken out of the den, and no manner of hurt was found upon him, because he believed his God" (Dan. 6:19-23).

After Daniel's ordeal, the king promoted Daniel and he prospered in the reign of king Darius. God would certainly deliver you when you are faced with the lion's den predicament. He will never allow His children to be destroyed by the forces of darkness. Your protection is in God and His deliverance will be upon you no matter what you face in life.

Chapter Thirteen

YOUR BLESSING IS NEARER THAN YOU THOUGHT

"What things soever ye desire, when ye pray, believe that ye receive them, and ye shall have them" (Mark 11:24).

Your blessing is really nearer to you than you thought and this is very true if you would just believe it. In actual fact, you have worked so hard at pursuing your dreams and goals and now everything you've believed God for is now about to unfold unto you. In short, you are now moving into the season of the manifestations of your vision and the sun is now on the horizon to shine forth unto you. Indeed, you have laboured all these years trying to realize your dreams and vision and everything is now coming together to work out for you. You know when a farmer plants seeds, he tends them and then waits for the harvest to arrive and when his harvest arrives, he begins to harvest joyfully. Your harvest is just a stone throw away and you are about to smile and praise the Lord your God.

God wants to crown all your labour with tremendous success and He wants you to be ready for it. A lot of times we labour and don't know for sure when the harvest will manifest but God is saying to you that the time has come for you to realize it. Life indeed is in seasons and we have spring, summer, autumn and winter and also we have day and night as well. Your waiting season is over and now is the time for you to reap with joy. Maybe you have laboured in the ministry all these years and you've been wondering when the harvest is coming, but the good Lord has declared that your harvest has just unfolded unto you and you need to embrace it and enjoy it.

Probably you have spent all these years setting up your business or ministry but right now you are moving into a new season of your harvest and every dryness in your life is giving way to fruitfulness. God always prepares a set time for the manifestation of your success and you need to look up for the sky is blue and the rain of your blessings is coming down to you. Maybe you've been in a terrible season of trials and tribulations, and it seems as though everything you've touched had been severely attacked, but right now there is a turn-around for you. The days of your struggles and sorrow are now over in your life and this is the beginning of a bright new season and divine release unto you.

A new thing is about to happen to you and you need to believe it. **"Remember ye not the former things, neither consider the things of old. Behold, I will do a new thing; now it shall spring forth; shall ye not know it? I will even make a way in the wilderness, and rivers in the desert"** (Isaiah 43:18&19).

God is now ready to do a new thing in your life and you need to believe it and position yourself for your blessings. God is now about to pour down His blessings unto you. You have tasted His blessings in the past and for some reason the devil attacked everything you had, but God says He is now about to release the rain and the latter rain together in your life. **"Be glad then, ye children of Zion, and rejoice in the LORD your God: for he hath given you the former rain moderately and he will cause to come down for you the rain, the former rain, and the latter rain in the first month. And the floors shall be full of wheat, and the fats shall overflow with wine and oil. And I will restore to you the years that the Locust hath eaten, the cankerworm, and the caterpillar, and the palmerworm, my great army which I sent among you. And ye shall eat in plenty, and be satisfied, and praise the name of the LORD your God that hath dealth wondrously with you: and my people shall never be ashamed. And ye shall know that I am in the midst of Israel, and that**

How to Succeed in Life

I am the LORD your God, and none else: and my people shall never be ashamed" (Joel 2:23-27).

The days of moderate blessings are over in your life and God will now be releasing an awesome blessing that you have not handled before. He will bless you to an overflow and you will not even have enough room to contain it. Your hard days are over and your days of struggle and not having enough are now a bygone story and you've just entered into a refreshing season of provision and abundance. The level of the attacks and trials you've been through has now qualified you for this enormous blessing that God is now releasing. In fact, because of the ferocity of your attacks you thought that the days of blessings in your life are over but God is reassuring you that you have just entered into the best season of your life. A new beginning has heralded in your life and for the next seasons to come, you will be more blessed than you have ever been in your whole life. God has now planted His fountain of blessing in you to bring you a continuous flow of His blessings. In short, God's blessings maketh rich and adds no sorrow to it (Prov. 10:22).

One good thing we need to understand is that God's blessings are continuously flowing towards us or past us every day and if we don't recognize it, we will miss it. God's blessings are flowing continuously and if we are not seeing it, then it means that the demonic powers are blocking it. Every hidden blessing of yours that has been kidnapped by the demonic forces, God is about to release them back to you right at this very moment. **"Thus saith the LORD to his anointed, to Cyrus, whose right hand I have holden, to subdue nations before him; and I will lose the loins of kings, to open before him the two leaved gate; and the gates shall not be shut: I will go before thee, and make the croaked places straight: I will break in pieces the gates of brass, and cut asunder the bars of iron: and I will give thee the treasures of darkness, and hidden riches of secret places, that thou mayest know that I, The LORD, which call thee by name, am the God of Israel"** (Isaiah 45:13)

There are a lot of hidden blessings in the storehouse of the demonic forces and these are the blessings of people who have opened doors for them to

Bishop Ben Ugbine

be attacked. Maybe the devil stole many things from you and have locked them up and you've struggled through all these years, but that is about to change. God is going to snatch every hidden blessing hidden in secret places and He is going to release them back to you so that your joy might be full.

The sky is full of rain

The cloud of your blessings are already full and it's about to rain down your blessings. You have sown into your dream, goals and vision and now all your efforts are about to be rewarded with an abundance of God's rain of blessings. I want you to know that God scheduled your blessings even before He put the vision inside of you and the rain of your blessing was predetermined from the beginning of time. God doesn't need to know anything from you to bless you. He knew you even before your mother conceived you and gave birth to you.

The sky is now blue and it is a sign that your blessings are about to be rained down. Prepare yourself and receive this blessing that God has prepared for you from the foundation of the world. **"If the clouds be full of rain, they empty themselves upon the earth: and if the tree fall towards the south, or towards the north, in the place where the tree falleth, there it shall be"** (Eccl. 11:3).

The scripture is talking about a season of sowing and a season of receiving. Our sowing might be into our vision or sowing financially into the things of God. Every time we sow a seed, the cloud of our blessings builds up and over a period of time, it will begin to rain down our blessings. And every blessing we receive is according to the seed that was sown. Every time we sow into our goals, dreams or vision, we are building up a momentum in the cloud and when that momentum is built up to a reasonable level, it begins to pour down blessings unto us.

Sowing is the consequent result of reaping. Everything in life is about sowing and reaping and when we sow hard work and dedication, it produces great reward onto us. If we want to see tangible things happen in our lives, then we need to begin to sow into our future. Your future is the sum total of all your seed sown. If you sow good seeds, then your future would produce good fruits for you. What you are currently sowing today is only preparing the way for your bright future. If we really want to change the outcome of our lives, then we have to take proper cognizant of what we sow in life. Nothing happens for nothing and everything we experience in life is as a result of what has been sown in the past.

Rebellion blocks blessings

Rebellion is a spirit that God hates and it closes every heavenly blessing from flowing into our lives. When we are rebellious to the instructions of God, it opens the way for the forces of darkness to hinder our blessings. Rebellion as a matter of fact causes stagnation in our lives and makes us to experience dryness financially, physically and spiritually. When we are willing and obedient to God, we will enjoy the good of the land. **"If ye be willing and obedient, ye shall eat the good of the land: but if ye refuse and rebel, ye shall be devoured with the sword: for the mouth of the LORD hath spoken it"** (Isaiah 1:19&20).

God's hand will be seen in your life when your life is dedicated to pleasing God rather than men.

Whatever instruction God gives you it must be carried out with every ounce of energy you have. He is the one that has the power to bless you like you've never been blessed before. A willing sheep is always obedient to his shepherd and it is the shepherd's responsibility to care for the sheep. You will be where God wants you to be if you will walk according to His ordinances and commandments. When your life is pleasing to God, He will cause even your enemies to be at peace with you.

The favour and power of God comes upon us when we walk in obedience. We must close the door of disobedience and rebellion to the devil and not give him any ounce of opportunity to hinder what God has in store for us. There is so much stuff God wants to release to us, but He's waiting for our obedience to come to par to walk into it. It's already been released but our rebellious attitude has hindered it from coming to us.

Bishop Ben Ugbine

Following God's way is actually the true way to walking in the abundance of God's blessings. Stay true to God's word and whatever He asks you to do, you need to do it with all humility. When we allow pride to come in and want to walk in our own ways, then the blessings of God will be denied us. The devil wants you to rebel but there is no need for that rather if we will walk in His will and commandments, surely His full blessings will come upon us.

Chapter Fourteen

THE POWER OF THE SPOKEN WORDS

"Death and life are in the power of the tongue: and they that love it shall eat the fruit thereof" (Prov. 18:21).

The words we speak out of our mouth are the determining factors to what flows into your life. Words are powerful and they go forth and bring into manifestation what we have professed. Be careful of what you say because it will come into manifestation. Your words must be guarded if you are to see good things come or happen to you. You cannot be negative with your words and expect good things to come to you. To see good things happen to you, then it is vital for you to change your confession. Death and life are in the power of your words and if you need to eat the fruit of your lips, then you will have to control what you say. When a person says 'I feel like I am sick' that person will suddenly become sick because of the power of their confession. Even though you might be feeling sick, you can turn things around if you hold on to a positive confession. Your confession has the power to change and turn things around. Words are powerful and they shape everything around us. We need to keep our words upbeat and let them direct and shape our lives to reflect what we really desire to become. Even when the situation looks dark and gloomy, we must speak what we want the situation to become. If we continue to speak what we are experiencing all the time, that will reinforce a stronghold in our lives, and cause that situation to persist for a long period of time.

Bishop Ben Ugbine

To be candid, there is going to be many dark moments in our lives but we must always remain positive and confess our victory. Negative words can really magnify something that is so small and make it look bigger and cause it to depress one's life. With powerful and reassuring words, you can make a mountain look like a molehill just by your spoken words. Your victory and deliverance over your dark moments, will be determined by how much you are able to hold on to your positive words of faith that can bring you out.

Positive words would attract things and people to you but negative words will drive them far away from you. You will not have people come around you if all that comes out of your mouth is foul and negative words. People are always drawn to people who can speak encouraging and reassuring words to help them to get through their dark moments. One fact we need to realize about people is that everyone no matter how good looking they may appear to be, or how beautifully dressed they might look, they still have some issues in their lives they are still wrestling with. And the last thing they want to hear is somebody who will add to their affliction with negative words.

We should endeavour to make our lives to be of some form of comfort to those who are in affliction. Before we open our mouth to speak to people, we should be conscious of the fact that people have struggles they are battling with and we should minimize their burdens rather than fuel it.

God gave you a mouth to speak forth words but He did not say we should use that mouth to bless Him and curse people. You cannot speak blessing and cursing at the same time. Your mouth must be sanctified and purified with the word of God because His word cleanses and purifies. When we put the word of God in our hearts on a daily basis, it will cause our hearts to be filled with words of hope and assurance. When our hearts are filled with the word of God, then our mouth will speak forth what is in our hearts because out of the abundance of the heart, the mouth will speak. **"O generation of vipers, how can ye, being evil, speak good things? For out of the abundance of the heart the mouth speaketh. A good man out of the good treasure of the heart bringeth forth good things:**

How to Succeed in Life

and an evil man out of the evil treasure bringeth forth evil things. But I say unto you, That every idle word that men shall speak, they shall give account thereof in the day of judgment. For by thy words thou shalt be justified, and by thy words thou shalt be condemned" (Matt. 12:34-37).

The evil man cannot speak forth good words because his heart is full of evil and that's what he will speak forth but the good man would always speak forth goodness. A tree is known by its fruit, that is, by what it produces. An apple tree would always produce apples and a mango tree would equally produce mangoes. There is no way a mango tree can produce apples because it's not in its nature to do that.

The best way to really know a person is to hear them speak for some few hours, and what they are in the inside would start coming out of their mouth. If for instance a person is a habitual liar, before he finishes talking to you he would lie and exaggerate things. Many times people's words betray them because they may say things that truly reflect their character. The best way to know a person's character is to see them get offended and who they really are would come out of them. A good man or woman when he or she is offended, would react with much caution but an evil person would explode and speak profanities.

For you to go far in life, you need to guide your words and always think twice before responding to somebody especially when in a state of anger. It is not a sin to be angry but it is a sin when your anger makes you lose control and you begin to speak profanities. **"Be ye angry, and sin not. Let not the sun go down upon your wrath: neither give place to the devil"** (Eph. 4:26&27).

Anger when allowed to fester, can lead to deadly consequences. Some people get angry and allow it to remain in their heart for days, months and even years and the devil uses it to destroy their lives. Anger is a terrible emotion and if it is not controlled, it could bring disastrous outcomes. Your anger must be controlled and not allowed to go on longer than it should. When you are offended, it is good to speak your mind to the person and

Bishop Ben Ugbine

let it go. Don't allow it to drag more than is necessary. Deal with the issue and let it go and let God take charge. If you take things into your hands the result might not be favourable. It is important for us to allow the spirit of God to take control of things and let the love of God flow out of us to others.

Speaking to your dry bones

Everybody has an area in his or her life that could be referred to as dry bones and these areas that are not fruitful but are stagnant, we need to prophesy to those areas and command them to be fruitful. When our lives are dry, everything we touch or do becomes listless and lifeless. Your dryness could be in your job and probably you have been doing the same job now for a long time without any progress or maybe you have been in the same position for years without any substantial progress or promotion. Or it could be that you are facing dryness in your marriage, or ministry or project and everything looks stagnant and no progress whatsoever. What you need to do is to speak life to that area and command it to receive the resurrection of God. If you don't speak life to it, then it will remain stagnant and continuously remain dry. When you speak to the situation with the authority of God, it must obey you and begin to move accordingly.

In the book of Ezekiel chapter thirty-seven God told Ezekiel to speak to the dry bones and command life to come into them. He told Ezekiel that these dry bones are all the whole house of the children of Israel and that they need life to come back into them. **"The hand of the LORD was upon me, and carried me out in the spirit of the LORD, and set me down in the midst of the valley which was full of bones, and caused me to pass by them round about: and, behold, there were very many in the open valley; and lo, they were very dry. And he said unto me, son of man, can these bones live? And I answered, O Lord God, thou knowest. Again he said unto me, Prophesy upon these bones, and say unto them, O ye dry bones, hear the word of the LORD. Thus saith the Lord God unto these bones; Behold, I will cause breath to enter into you, and ye shall live: and I will lay sinews upon you, and will bring up**

90

How to Succeed in Life

flesh upon you, and cover you with skin, and ye shall know that I am the LORD. So I prophesied, there was a noise, and behold a shaking, and the bones came together, bone to his bones" (Ezek. 37:1-7).

God told Ezekiel to prophesy to the dry bones to receive flesh and sinews and when he did they responded to his words of authority. God wants us to always speak to our situation to receive life and your word has authority if you will believe it. There is no dry situation in your life that cannot respond to the words of authority. God has given us the authority and power to command situations to straighten up and they will obey.

Ezekiel believed God's word and he spoke it by faith to the dry bones and they obeyed his words. I decree right now that every area in your life that is dry to receive power and to rise again. In your marriage I command every dryness to seize and also I command every demonic power that has caused this dryness to let go right now. Maybe your project or vision has continuously remained dry and stagnant, I command it to move ahead in Jesus' name.

From this day forward there shall be a turn around and life will come back to your situation again. The power of God is able to revive things and I decree that revival to take place right now. Your dryness is over and the power of God has now turned things around for you and you will begin to see things speed up in your life from this time forth.

Chapter Fifteen

WHERE THERE IS A VISION – SUCCESS IS SURE

"For the vision is yet for an appointed time, but at the end it shall speak, and not lie: though it tarry, wait for it; because it will surely come, it will not tarry" (Hab. 2:3).

Vision is the ability to see into the future what God has already accomplished for you. When God gives a vision of things He wants accomplished in your life, you know that it is what He has already done from the foundation of the world. A vision is a finished assignment from God and most times when this vision is given, it can be very frightening because from where you are and where you need to go is just too far apart.

Usually when we are given a vision to bring to pass, we normally don't have the resources to make it happen and this sometimes overwhelms one. When God gives one a vision of something to do, He knows that we can make it if we trust Him to do it. God wants us to believe Him every inch of the way to bring it to pass. If we want to figure it out how we can make it happen, then it will look impossible but if God becomes the propeller of the vision, you can be sure that it will come to pass.

Anytime God gives one a vision of something great to accomplish, the forces of darkness would mount an attack against you to try to abort

How to Succeed in Life

the vision but we must resist him and trust God to fulfil the vision. One of the areas that the devil and his forces always like to attack first is the finances to make the vision not to happen. He would do anything to make sure that you don't have the money to carry the vision out and you know that without adequate money, no vision can be fulfilled. We must not be moved when there seem to be no money to fulfil the vision. We have to continuously trust and believe God by faith to provide the money to bring the vision into reality. For instance, God might give one a vision to build a new sanctuary for Him and that sanctuary might cost several millions of dollars or pounds to make it happen, and we wonder how that could possibly happen since one had not even handled a million dollar in one's life. If you approach things from the natural stand point you will be frustrated and discouraged about the whole vision. When God gives a vision, He never gives you what you can achieve by your own self. In fact, He always wants you to believe Him for the money to buy the building. Indeed He wants us to walk by faith and begin to call the things that be not as though they were. He wants us to trust Him for the provision and if we do, miracles will certainly happen before our eyes.

There have been men and women who have had visions that cost millions of dollars and they believed God for the money and by His miraculous power, He provided the money for the vision. We must understand that a vision is for an appointed time and it is not something that usually happens over-night. There is always a fixed time for the maturation of the vision and even if the vision is delayed wait for it and don't give up. Sometimes we tend to get so discouraged so quickly if the vision doesn't happen at the time we want it to happen. But we must endeavour to be patient and wait for the right time for God to bring the vision to pass. Though it tarries wait for it for it must surely come to pass.

What God has scheduled and predetermined from the foundation of the world, must come to pass. The enemy might fight the vision but God would certainly bring it to pass. He would not allow the devil to abort the vision for He will uphold you and make the vision happen. God knows that He can trust you with the vision hence He gave it to you. Be rest

Bishop Ben Ugbine

assured that you have a Jehovah-jireh who would make every provision available to you to carry out the vision.

God knows how to touch the hearts of men to sow into your vision. One thing about a vision is that even though the vision is given to one man, it needs many people to bring the vision to pass. You need men and women who will believe the vision and help you to fulfil it. When we attempt to do by ourselves what others have to be involved in, we frustrate ourselves and delay the vision. When a vision is given, we must try to sell the vision to others so that they can run with the vision. The vision must be written down and made plain so that those who read it can run with it. When a vision is written down, it becomes articulated and alive and real to one. It is a known fact that those who write down their vision stands a better chance of seeing the vision come into fulfilment. Writing the vision down is really making a statement that one truly believes in the vision and that one is determined to make it come into reality.

Vision needs focus and persistence to make it come to pass. If one is distracted from the vision that could allow the enemy to abort it. It is extremely important to put the vision before you where you can always see it and be inspired. We need to stay inspired on the vision at all times. It must be something you are always thinking about. The more you think about the vision, the more it grows in you and the quicker you see it come to pass.

A lot of times, our vision will bring us into a wilderness experience where everything seems dry and difficult. Actually this is the point where many people lose focus on their vision because they are facing very trying times that they are going through. It is very significant to always focus on the vision even when we find ourselves in the wilderness. The devil wants to kill the vision and he will try to torment your mind in your wilderness and make you feel like all hope is lost and gone. Do not allow him to remove your eyes from the vision because the vision is the motivating force that would energize you to come out of the wilderness. In short, most people's visions are usually killed during their wilderness experiences. Since these are very difficult and trying times for one when everything seems to be

How to Succeed in Life

going against one, the devil uses it as an opportunity to destroy the vision. When our focus is on the vision even in our trying moment, God would make a way for us to overcome it and fulfil our vision. A lot of times when the fulfilment of the vision is coming to its maturation, the attacks on you seem to get intensified but if you would hold on without giving in, you will come out with tremendous breakthroughs. No vision that one receives from God is without an attack from the enemy. In fact, most of the terrible experiences one tends to go through comes when a vision is given to them. The devil is always afraid of a vision because he knows something glorious will come out of it that would bring glory to God and he would do anything to try to destroy it. The devil and his forces hates anything good and when they see something awesome about to be done, they put up a stiff fight and opposition against it. But no matter how much the devil and his forces would want to fight, let us be reassured that we are on the winning side.

Your vision must certainly come to pass and the devil cannot abort it. Certainly he will fight the vision but he cannot abort it. If God be for you who can be against you? Certainly nobody can be against you. You are a winner and you have the backings of the Holy Spirit and the host of His holy angels guiding and helping to bring your vision into reality.

The kingdom of heaven suffereth violence and the violent must take it by force. You need the force of God to make your vision come to manifestation and if you have to put up a stiff fight against the devil and his forces, then do that and get your victory. **"And from the days of John the Baptist until now the kingdom of heaven suffereth violence, and the violent take it by force"** (Matt. 11:12).

We need the force of prayer to remove every obstacle that tends to hinder our vision. Prayer is one activity that destroys and frustrates all the plans of the enemy against our vision. Jesus Himself used the force of prayer to destroy every plan the devil had to stop Him from carrying out His vision. His vision was to go to the cross and redeem mankind from the shackles of sin and bring them closer to God. The devil tried every way even after His birth to kill Jesus but he couldn't and even when Jesus was crucified,

Bishop Ben Ugbine

he tried to completely destroy Him but Jesus overcame him through the power of prayer. Prayer is the key to sustaining any vision and bringing it to pass and if we give ourselves to prayer we will achieve tremendous things for God.

Running with your vision

It is vital for us to keep on running with our vision until it is fulfilled. Your vision came from God and it is your job to keep the vision alive and even when the vision becomes stale or cold, we need to put some fire into it again. Many times the enthusiasm and the passion we have for the vision might run cold probably because of lack of money or something, but we must make sure that the vision remains alive. Visions can be aborted or lost just because we refuse to fire it up. We need to put more coal in the fire to keep it burning. The most dangerous thing that can happen to a person is for the fire of their vision to die out and when that happens, one becomes despondent and disillusioned. There are so many things in life that distracts one and we often face problems here and there and even sometimes there appears to be nobody to encourage one and this can quench the passion for the vision. But in spite of what happens around us, we must keep the vision alive and continue to run with it. A runner when he continues to run against all odds, stands the chance of finishing the race and possibly win but if he quits half way, there is no way he can finish or win. God wants you to keep on running and keep on encouraging yourself. When there is no one to encourage you encourage yourself and run on until you win. Life is not about how fast you finish but how well you run. You may run so fast and finish before everybody but if you don't run according to the rules, you will be disqualified even though you finished first. So we must run well to win and let God encourage us to run well and finish well.

"Know ye not that they which run in a race run all, but one receiveth the prize? So run, that ye may obtain. And every man that striveth for the mastery is temperate in all things. Now they do it to obtain a corruptible crown; but we an incorruptible. I therefore so run, not as uncertain; so fight I, not as one that beateth the air: but I keep

How to Succeed in Life

under my body, and bring it into subjection: lest that by any means, when I have preached to others, I myself should be a castaway" (1 Cor. 9:24-27).

We need to run with our vision with patience and be confident that the vision will be realized and not allow anything to hinder our running. A lot of self-discipline is required when one is running especially if one truly wants to win. A true winner is one who goes through a rigorous training and perseverance. Perseverance is an asset to someone with a vision who really wants to see his vision to come to pass. Even when one feels like quitting, one has to persevere and keep on running until one fulfils one's dreams and vision. Your vision is waiting for your arrival so don't stop but keep on running until you arrive to be greeted by your vision.

Chapter Sixteen

BREAKING THE BARRIER OF GENERATIONAL CURSES

"Christ hath redeemed us from the curse of the law, being made a curse for us; for it is written, Cursed is every one that hangeth on a tree: that the blessing of Abraham might come on the Gentiles through Jesus Christ; that we might receive the promise of the spirit through faith" (Gal. 3:13&14).

Curses are the devil's tools of blocking people's blessings and progress. When a curse is on someone, then the blessings becomes blocked and they would struggle and struggle through life without making any progress at all. Many don't seem to progress in life because they are under a curse. A curse comes on someone for many different reasons. When somebody treats somebody else in an unjust way, curses come on them. A curse can come on somebody too when they break a covenant that was binding. For instance, if a man and a woman made a covenant not to break a relationship and one of the partners breaks the covenant, a curse can come on that person. Curses can also be inherited. When a family is involved in so much evil every member of that family can be under a curse. Curses also come on a person who commits abortion or rebels against the word of God. In life nothing happens without a cause. This is always the reason why things happen, because what one has sown in one's life is exactly what one is going to reap. **"As the bird by wandering, as the swallow by flying, so the curse causeless shall not come"**(Prov. 26:2).

When a curse is on somebody, they would go through series of calamities in their life and labour fruitlessly without any achievable progress. A curse is simply an authority given to the forces of darkness to afflict and hinder your life. Witches and wizards also release curses on people. They put a curse on you and cause everything you do to end up in failure.

Most calamities that happen in people's lives are the work of witches and wizards. These forces of darkness are specialist in destroying people's blessings. Witches and wizards are enemies of progress and anywhere they smell blessings and success, they would try to destroy it. This is the reason why God hates witches because they are enemies of good things. **"Thou shalt not suffer a witch to live"** (Ex. 22:18).

Witches likes to destroy the work of people's hands and even destroy lives. We must pray vehemently against the activities of witches and wizards if we are to succeed with our dreams and visions. But one thing we have to realize is that if we are covered by the blood of the Lamb, no evil power can overcome us. God's power is greater than the forces of witches and wizards and we don't have to fear them rather we should take authority over them. Your life is hidden in Christ and in God and for them to get you, they have to get Jesus first and that can't happen. God's divine covering and protection is over those who hide under Him as their refuge. **"He that dwelleth in the secret place of the Most High shall abide under the shadow of the Almighty. I will say of the LORD, He is my refuge and my fortress: my God, in him will I trust"** (Psalm 91:1&2).

To break a curse from your life, you need to repent from the sin that brought the curse and wash yourself with the blood of the Lamb. When your sin is not confessed and revoked, the curse continues to operate in one's life. When the sin is confessed, then we ask God to break it by the power of His anointing. The anointing of God can destroy every curse and stop its operation in your life. **"And it shall come to pass in that day, that his burden shall be taken away from off thy shoulder and**

Bishop Ben Ugbine

the yoke from off thy neck, and the yoke shall be destroyed because of the anointing" (Isaiah 10:27).

One of the most predominant curses that operate in people's lives is generational curses. These are inherited curses from parents or grant parents or generations past. Most families under the face of the earth are under curses and that is because that family has been involved in terrible evil that have given the demonic powers the legal ground to operate. People are affected by generational curses because they are linked to their families by blood. Just as people can inherit their parent's illness or attributes even so they can inherit their curses as well. You may not have committed the sin that brought the curse but because you are related to them by blood, it begins to affect your life and the same applies to blessings as well. When a family is blessed everyone in that family inherits it. Because Abraham was blessed by God all his seed becomes automatically blessed too. A curse can run for hundreds and hundreds of years if not broken. It goes from one generation to another generation and retards and hinders that family. **"Thou shalt have no other gods before me. Thou shalt not make unto thee any graven image, or any likeness of anything that is in heaven above, or that is in the earth beneath, or that is in the water under the earth: thou shalt not bow down thyself to them, nor serve them: for I the LORD thy God am a jealous God, visiting the iniquity of the fathers upon the children unto the third and fourth generation of them that hates me"** (Ex. 20:3-5).

Generational curses can be broken under deliverance and under the anointing. Generational curses affect every member of the family whether they know about it or not. This curse is much stronger in a family of idol worshippers and witchcraft operations. A family that is rooted in witchcraft will know no progress and they will always have one calamity from the other happening to each and every members of the family. Some of them can go through childlessness or suffer from a terrible incurable disease or sickness.

God wants us to move forward and progress and fulfil our purpose and vision but if we have curses operating in our lives it will no doubt hinder

How to Succeed in Life

one. The best thing to do is to seek for deliverance and let the curse and the yoke be broken. My book entitled, 'The Power of Deliverance' can be of tremendous help to you in this regard. You can order it online at <u>www.authorhouse.com</u> or call 1-800 839 8640 in the States and in the UK you can order it online at <u>www.authorhouse.co.uk</u> or call 1-800 197 4150.

Your vision is too important and powerful for you not to fulfil it. So if you are being affected by generational curses that is hindering your life, let the anointing power of God break it for you. When the anointing of God touches your life, every curse will be removed from your life and your blessings will begin to flow unto you.

The blood of Jesus is so potent that no curse can stand before it. Let the blood of Jesus overshadow your life and it will break and revoke every curse from your life. Jesus shed His blood on Calvary to give you victory and we need to cover ourselves at all times with His blood. **"And they overcame him by the blood of the Lamb, and by the word of their testimony; and they loved not their lives unto the death"** (Rev. 12:11).

Demons of limitations

There are demons that are sent out into the world to limit those who are under a curse. A woman can be under a curse and would have six children for five different men and not be married to any of them and this pattern might run through all the female children in that family. There are families that might be under the curse of divorce and everyone that marries in that family after a few years of marriage it ends up in divorce. Some families might be wealthy and after awhile, the wealth disappears mysteriously and everyone in that family flows in that same pattern. This is the spirit of limitations in operation and this spirit causes misery and sorrow in people's lives.

When a person is limited, their progress will continuously be frustrated by demons. The demons of limitations are usually wasteful demons and their job is to waste your resources and your life. A family can be under this spirit and nobody in that family can live up to the age of forty or

Bishop Ben Ugbine

fifty. When they are near that age, something unexplainable happens and they die.

This spirit can drain one's money and make one to be in serious debt or live in abject poverty. The spirit of limitation is a poverty spirit and it causes one to borrow a lot of money and waste it and be unable to pay it back and live in sorrow.

If your life is not progressing and you have a vision that seems unrealizable, you might be suffering from the spirit of limitation. If you are married and you have never known one day of peace, you might be under the spirit of limitation. If you've been married for years and you find it impossible to be pregnant, you may be under the spirit of limitation. Whatever condition you might be in that is frustrating your life, know that God is able to set you free.

You need to come boldly to the throne of grace and receive help from the Lord. The Lord knows your infirmities and He will set you free from them. He whom the son of man shall set free shall be free indeed. You can be free and have this spirit broken from your life so that you can realize your dreams and vision and fulfil them.

I decree right now that every spirit of limitation holding you bound I command it to be broken and I charge you to move forward with your life. You are redeemed of God and the devil and his demons have no authority or power to depress your life. The dreams and visions that God has put in the inside of you will surely come to pass, and you will see it happen in no time at all. Yes, you've been through hell and high waters but your season of breakthroughs and deliverance has just arrived. The devil has hindered your life for years but today I put a stop to that and I command you to rise up and begin to move forward and do things. I command every generational curse to be broken from your life and that of your family in Jesus' name. I undo every evil that has been programmed into your life and I terminate the assignments of the demonic powers to let you go. Just as Jesus spoke to Lazarus to come forth, even so I command you to come forth from every depression, sorrow, and barrenness and be what God has

How to Succeed in Life

ordained you to be. Devil, I speak to you right now that your authority and assignment is over and this life will begin to shine and succeed. So expect great things in your life from this time forth. You have been loosed and the anointing power of God has now come upon you to succeed in life. Today will mark a new era in your life because God is going to release some blessings you have never seen before in your life. Today is really the day of your deliverance and something remarkable has just happened to you.

CHAPTER SEVENTEEN

HAVING THE WINNING ATTITUDE

"When you focus your mind on winning, every obstacle will disappear from your way and nothing will be able to stop you from achieving your dreams" (Bishop Ben Ugbine).

To really win in life attitude plays a great role indeed. If you are actually going to win in life, you need to have the right attitude to really be a true winner. Nobody wins in life if they have a cavalier attitude towards everything. You will only win when your mind-set is on winning and when you have that kind of mind-set, nothing can stop you from winning. Winning is an attitude and until we understand that, we will wonder why people around us are winning and we are not.

If an athlete has a double mind before running a race, you can be sure that they will not win that race. Winning begins from the mind and you can't feel defeat in your mind and expect to win. Life is made up of winners and losers and the difference between a winner and a loser is how they think in their mind. You can win a race just in your mind and then express it outwardly.

The right mental approach to things is very crucial in life otherwise one cannot have the victory one should have. A double minded man is not fixed in his ways. **"A double minded man is unstable in all his ways"** (Jas. 1:8).

How to Succeed in Life

The things you have in your mind to do in life can be achieved, and you need to believe that they are achievable and trust God to make them happen, and certainly they will happen. What you don't want to happen to you is to be double minded or waver in your belief concerning what you want to do or achieve. No matter what your desires are just know that you can make them come to reality. Is it to be married? You can achieve it. Is it to travel around the world? You can do it if you set your mind on it. Your dream can definitely come true and you need to believe it. It might look impossible but work with the God of all possibilities and He will make miracles out of you.

Your destiny is calling you and you need to respond to it. Who can stop you from climbing up the mountain top? Certainly nobody and the mountain is all yours. Those who have climbed to the top of Mount Everest believed that they could and set up their mind to believe it and had the right attitude before setting out to climb. Climbing Mount Everest can certainly be an overwhelming and daunting task, but people have climbed to the top because they believed they could. You can climb to the top of your carrier or profession and become victorious if you would work on your thinking and know that you can do it successfully.

Being a winner is a wonderful experience and it can build up one's moral and confidence too but we have to learn how to sustain that attitude so that we can remain winners. Sometimes in life, we can't always win and every now and then we might lose, but we must learn from the experience and use it as a launching pad for our next victory. When we do lose in whatever we are doing, it is important not to give up but we must try over and over again until we win. Never quit until you win. If you have to do things over again by all means do it but don't you ever quit. Quitters don't win and winners don't quit.

God from the beginning of time had your best interest at heart and He wants you to succeed and come on top and if God believes in you, of course you have to believe in yourself. If nobody believes in your ability you better believe in yourself and if you bring yourself to doing that then you will win.

105

Bishop Ben Ugbine

The joy of success

Success comes when our dreams are fully realized and it brings ample joy into our lives. Just as losing demoralizes one, success motivates one to forge ahead and do more. When we win and our dreams and visions mature and come to fruition, it gladdens our hearts and makes us rejoice. Your joy will be full when the blessings of God overtakes your life and everything seems to be going on okay in your life.

Dreams do come true and visions will also come to its fulfilment at its set time. There is time for everything in life and when the time for one's vision comes, there is no force that can stop it from happening. When God has destined one to be blessed nothing can ever hinder it. God wants our lives to be full of joy hence He keeps speaking to us about His blessings.

Jesus said the devil came to steal, to kill and to destroy but I have come to give you life, and to give it more abundantly. Abundant life means a life of overflow and continuous blessing. When God wants to bless you, He blesses you to an overflow. God takes delight in blessing His people and no one who trusts in Him goes unblessed.

Your God is Jehovah–jireh and He delights in blessing His children. Every father delights in blessing His children especially if they are obedient to Him. Because we've been walking in the ordinances of God, He has set aside many blessings for us.

Success like I mentioned earlier on in this book is not a destination but a journey and it is important to enjoy every segment of the journey. Success is a conglomeration of different completed assignments. What is success for one person, might not necessarily be success for the next person. Success for one person might be driving to work every morning and to another, success might be buying a house or buying a car. Whatever success is to you it is important that you enjoy it. When one success is built upon another success, it creates an atmosphere of gladness and joy and that's what keeps the spirit of man passionately motivated.

How to Succeed in Life

Success makes life worth living

When we are successful in what we do life becomes meaningful and beautiful and everything around us begins to blossom. The sky becomes bluer and everything around us begins to bubble with life and excitement. When people are not achieving any success in what they do, then life becomes uninteresting and everything around them becomes dull and dry.

Obviously the successful fulfilment of one's vision and dreams makes one look forward to another day of work. When someone enjoys what they do, time seems to run that fast but if they are not enjoying it, time tends to drag on forever and this could make them unhappy and unfulfilled too.

We have to fulfil our purpose and fulfilling it engenders peace and true happiness. As a matter of fact, the greatest desire of every man on earth is to be happy and they would do what it takes to produce that happiness. For instance, when two people get married their intention is for them to be happy but we all know that being married does not guarantee that happiness. When people buy themselves a car the ultimate result is for them to be happy but having a car could bring them unhappiness. Material things per se cannot produce happiness. The only sure way to have happiness and joy is to live a life that is well pleasing to God. Happiness, peace and joy come from the Lord and He is the source of it all. Our lives will be tremendously enhanced if we give ourselves totally and completely to the Lord and we should know that He's the author and the beginner of our peace.

People focus most times on material things to give them happiness but many have been so distraught that the happiness and joy they think material things will produce for them never happened. Many have even committed suicide because of the deep depression and hopelessness they felt inside. The true journey to happiness is walking closely with the Lord Himself. Indeed, the journey within will bring one all the joy and happiness one truly desires. I do strongly believe that true success in life comes from walking the spiritual and mystical life. The inner life as opposed to the outward life is the journey to God and self-realization. Every mystic

Bishop Ben Ugbine

who has achieved true happiness received it only when they renounced the mundane life for the spiritual life. A life of the spiritual journey to self-realization will definitely open the door to spiritual emancipation and truth. Knowing the truth of God's word and living it will produce harmony and peace of mind in one's life and then one can be said to be successful. A relationship with the divine creator is the best gift one can give oneself and it is the greatest achievement one can ever make in life. When one's soul is in union with God, you know for sure that one would experience all the joy and peace of mind one could ever imagine in their life, and that to me is the journey to true success and spiritual power.

As we come to the end of this book and I would like to encourage you to give life all you've got. The world is at your reach and nothing in this world can stop you from achieving your dreams and visions. Give your dreams or visions 100% focus and do not allow anything else to distract you. Your dream can certainly come to pass and you have what it takes to make it happen. Believe in yourself and also believe in God and both of you as partners can never fail. You are a winner and your victory is just around the corner. No matter what you face in life on your way to the realization of your dream or vision, don't you ever quit. As you know, winners don't quit and quitters don't win and when the going gets tough the tough gets going. And I also want you to realize that tough times don't last only tough people do.

I want you to know for sure that no matter how big your dream or vision might be God can help you to realize it. Believe in your dream and believe also in yourself. What seems impossible with men is indeed possible with God. You can make it and don't you ever give up in your struggle to make it. I do believe that within the shortest possible time you will celebrate your success and all the praise and glory will definitely be ascribed to God who is the architect of all good things in life. Congratulations you are indeed a winner and you are also a success story to the world and God has really smiled on you. Go ahead and enjoy your success and also share it with the world. You have laboured much and now you've achieved your dream and your heart's desires and happiness and joy are now your portion. Glory be to God in the highest who is able to do exceeding, abundantly above all that we could ever ask or think.

FOR FURTHER ENQUIRIES

If this book has been of tremendous blessing to you why not send me an email and let me know about it. Send your email to bishopbenugbine@yahoo.com or telephone me in (Nigeria) 08039141254, (Outside Nigeria) +2348039141254, In UK +447469926160
Facebook:
Facebook.com/bishopbenugbine

<u>Church Address:</u>

House of Faith Mission Int.
7 Prince Babatunde Adefioye Street, Off Lawn Tennis Club,
Junction B/Stop, by Splash Water,
Jakande Estate, Oke-Afa, Lagos Nigeria

UK Address
Flat 2, macnamaras Court, 2 Palmerston Road,
Ipswich, Suffolk, IP4 2LN, England

Lightning Source UK Ltd.
Milton Keynes UK
UKHW040107311218
334744UK00001B/22/P